How to Negotiate Effectively

How to Negotiate Effectively

David Oliver | Third Edition

LONDON PHILADELPHIA NEW DELHI

Publisher's note

Every possible effort has been made to ensure that the information contained in this book is accurate at the time of going to press, and the publishers and author cannot accept responsibility for any errors or omissions, however caused. No responsibility for loss or damage occasioned to any person acting, or refraining from action, as a result of the material in this publication can be accepted by the editor, the publisher or the author.

Parts of this book were previously published as *101 Ways to Negotiate More Effectively*, also published by Kogan Page.
First published as *How to Negotiate Effectively* in 2003
Reprinted 2004, 2005
Second edition 2006
Reprinted 2007, 2008
Third edition 2011

120 Pentonville Road
London N1 9JN
United Kingdom
www.koganpage.com

525 South 4th Street, #241
Philadelphia PA 19147
USA

4737/23 Ansari Road
Daryaganj
New Delhi 110002
India

ISBN 978 0 7494 6170 6
E-ISBN 978 0 7494 6135 5

British Library Cataloguing in Publication Data

A CIP record for this book is available from the British Library.

Library of Congress Cataloging-in-Publication Data

Oliver, David, 1951-
How to negotiate effectively / David Oliver. -- 3rd ed.
p. cm.
ISBN 978-0-7494-6134-8 -- ISBN 978-0-7494-6135-5 (ebk) 1. Negotiation in businesss. 2. Negotiation. I. Title.
HD58.6.O38 2011
658.4052--dc22

2010018064

Typeset by Jean Cussons Typesetting, Diss, Norfolk
Printed and bound in India by Replika Press Pvt Ltd

This book is dedicated to my dad, who taught me my first steps in negotiation. He taught me the work ethic and showed me by example how to love hard work.

Contents

Introduction

This book is for you!

If you are in buying or selling, a business owner or manager, this book is likely to dramatically change your world and your results. Everyone in business invariably both buys and sells. Most business owners, managers and partners buy and sell in different ways every week, sometimes every day. This book is for you, to help you get the best out of every deal, whether it's a one-off deal or a long-term relationship. It is also for the professional salesman or buyer.

Each of these keys for better negotiation has been specifically written so that it has application for selling and buying. Apply the principles in this book and you should quite easily see an improvement in your net profit of at least 10 per cent. No, I'm not exaggerating, so please don't switch off! Just one idea alone has saved me £10,000 on the purchase of our family boat.

In fact, in 20 years of teaching this material, no one I know has ever lost money as a result of its application. But hundreds of people that I have heard from have taken one or more of these keys and achieved better deals time and time again.

The material in this book is useful in every sphere of life – work and family. For example one of our kids works as a trainee paramedic. She has to negotiate with difficult patients and the ambulance dispatcher from the control centre.

Husbands and wives often unwittingly negotiate. Families negotiate in relationships and in the parent–children roles – especially in the teenage years. Our youngest daughter is in the middle of buying her first starter home and that is a huge negotiation at a young age.

Very few business people negotiate effectively, and the rewards for those who do are great. Follow these principles and above-average performance will follow. A 10 per cent improvement is well within your grasp, so read on!

One trend today in modern business practice is based around partnerships between suppliers and customers. To enjoy a long-term relationship, both buyer and seller must reach mutual agreement about the business being transacted – not just price but a whole range of terms, conditions and other related ingredients. To do that, they negotiate. The skill of the negotiators will determine whether that relationship succeeds or fails. The greater your skill, the greater the advantage you can expect.

The bulk of examples and anecdotes in this book are from a business setting. The principles underpinning them however are transferable into family and workplace relationships.

Many of you reading this book will have ideas or examples of your own. I would love to hear from you. Why not write to me at Kogan Page – maybe I can use your anecdote in the next edition!

1

Definition

Know what negotiation is

There are many misconceptions about negotiation. Estate agents like to call themselves 'negotiators', yet in house sales they rarely do anything, except discount the price of the property. Many salespeople describe themselves as negotiators. So what is it? Is it a Dutch auction, which starts high and goes lower? Is it another word for selling? These are very common misconceptions. In fact, negotiation is none of these. A simple dictionary definition describes negotiation as 'discussing or bargaining in order to reach agreement'.

Negotiation is a transaction in which both parties have a veto on the final outcome. It requires voluntary consent on both sides. It is a give and take process where the actual conditions of a transaction are agreed. It is the act or process of bargaining to reach a mutually acceptable agreement or objective. It requires movement on both sides – real or perceived.

Why do we negotiate? Simply because if we don't we will not get the best deals available to us. One thing I can promise you is:

if you don't negotiate, you are already losing money or missing out on the best outcome. The reality is, of course, that lots of people in business do not negotiate – they simply make agreements the best they can and it costs them every single time. A senior manager from one of the world's leading software companies called me and said this: '*Reading your material, I realised that our team of sellers never negotiate, they just close the deal. We are losing large sums of money every month just because no one has taught us a better way. Can you come and help us?*'

In a free market economy there are only two pivots around which any deal will finally be agreed: price and value. The bulk of people in business concentrate just on price – wrongly. Focus just on price and the best deals will never come your way.

Negotiation is in some ways like chess. You are prepared to sacrifice particular pieces in the interests of winning the game. In chess you know the pieces but you can't see into the other person's mind. In negotiation you don't necessarily know the 'pieces'. You have to discover and develop your own pieces and find ways of uncovering your counterparts'.

Know what negotiation isn't

Negotiation is not selling. That is a mistaken assumption and one that was made by the software company we just mentioned. Negotiation begins when the sale has been adequately made.

The simple test is the way buyer and seller relate to each other. In the selling phase, one person is persuading, the other is being persuaded. In true negotiation, the attitude of both is the same – both want to reach agreement. The question is no longer whether to buy or not. The question becomes, 'On what terms can I buy or sell?' Negotiation assumes that there is already an established desire to buy and an ability to supply. The whole emphasis moves towards profit implications and specific terms or arrangements.

Salespeople frequently fail to realise when the role of seller changes to that of negotiator, and it costs them. I asked scores of people for anecdotes on negotiation. Most of the salespeople struggled to find one. Many of them said, 'I do it intuitively.' When I questioned them in detail, the truth was that they did not recognise this transition from selling to negotiation. As a result, in every case they were not effective.

Negotiation is not 'giving in' or conceding. Concession can imply surrender on another person's terms. If we view negotiation as surrendering it will condition our thinking, our approach will be weak and our deals will not be effective. That does not mean we won't move in our negotiation – we will. But our movement must never be giving in or moving 'one way'.

Negotiation is not about digging our heels in. If we are inflexible we will be met by equal inflexibility. Showing our strength and wanting to appear tough are not the same as good negotiation. They can reflect our own insecurity and will either lead to immediate deadlock, or they will be exploited by our counterpart, and rightly so. Negotiation doesn't just relate to agreeing terms in the buying process, it can relate to a whole variety of issues such as disputed ownership or late/non-payment.

Win–win

A number of possibilities exist about the way we view the negotiation process. The moderately aggressive stance is where we look out primarily for a strong gain for ourselves. The win–win concept is where we look for our best interest, but where we understand that the other person's interests, if served well, can often serve ours even better. To be effective, both parties must feel they have won.

I was introduced to this personally when one of my clients asked me to launch a company. He never offered me a salary; he asked me to write my own proposal, taking into account the fact that he wanted me to be as motivated as possible to get the best possible return for him as investor. Not only did it force certain issues in my own thinking, it put a strong sense of responsibility on my shoulders. My client looked at the proposal I made, and found one or two places where he believed he could improve my motivation – he was right.

What are the possible attitudes available in a negotiation process?

1. I win you lose – here I must defeat the other party at any cost. I drive a hard bargain, I probably don't trust anyone. I don't care about the relationship.
2. I yield when you press – here I believe that good relationship is what produces good deals and the relationship is the most important thing to me. I trust without reservation and I yield to pressure.
3. I withdraw. Here I have low interest in the relationship and the outcome. I lack confidence and belief. I feel powerless, results are beyond my influence and I take what ever is willingly conceded.
4. I compromise. Similar to number 2, here I have a reasonable degree of concern for both the outcome and the relationship. I will tend to split the difference, I will go out of my way to scratch their back and I accept that you win some and you lose some.
5. I want Win–Win. Relationship is important to me but not at the cost of achieving my goals. I will genuinely search for common interest as well as looking for synergistic creative solutions.

Good negotiation is not about getting everything your own way. It is about balancing each other. You don't defer to your counterpart and concede all that he or she wants – you have your own aspirations, which you must secure. That requires *two-way movement which produces win–win*. It affects the business relationship positively. It also enables us to achieve not just more sales or better supply, but more importantly, the growth in profit that we are all looking for.

In effective negotiation we should not only be concerned about our own goals and objectives. We should have a genuine interest in, and a good grasp of, what the other party is hoping for or aiming for. The more we can help the other party to achieve what they want, the more likely we are to achieve what we are looking for from the deal. Some trainers assert that you should focus on your own position only. The logic behind this is that the other party is the only one who knows what is best for them. That is probably true with skilled negotiators, but with inexperienced negotiators genuine two-way concern is often necessary.

The more genuine interest we can show in the other party and their aspirations, the less threatened they will be, the more they will volunteer information and the more likely we are to reach an ideal solution. If you can think *win–win* rather than *win–lose* you will become more effective, less stressed and always better in the long term.

A small software developer who worked for his client for two or three years graphically illustrated this. It seemed that at every opportunity, the client would try to screw more discount, more value, more price reductions. The software developer got fed up with the approach and allowed his feelings to dictate his response. He dug his heels in, and focused on his own interests. The result was alienation. Had there been frank dialogue, if both parties could have thought through what was important to the other, an amicable and profitable solution would have easily been found.

Count the cost

Great gain is to be had from negotiating, but only if the task is done effectively. There is a cost in terms of resolve, priorities, time, preparation, forward planning. At the heart of effective negotiation there has to be a calculation of what is involved and the price has to be paid, usually before the negotiation begins.

When I train I use the word *COST* as an acronym. It acts as a useful memory jog, reminding us of the four ingredients that represent the practical outworking of the cost involved: Commitment, Objective, Strategy, Tactics.

Commitment

Commitment to the negotiation process is required. This applies to negotiation as an overall process. It also applies specifically to a particular negotiation in hand. A half-hearted approach can never be effective in negotiation. There must be a serious commitment to achieving the result you want. If you are serious then you will be taken seriously; if you are casual then you will be taken casually.

In my experience, most business people do not have true commitment to the negotiation process. What typically happens is that negotiation gets the odd few moments, the remnants of our time. To be effective we need to settle the issue that negotiation is going to require predetermined amounts of time and resource.

Overall commitment

We must determine overall what our business goals are, and determine what levels of profit, volume, price, saving or improvement we are aiming for. This requires thinking through the key areas.

Commitment to a particular negotiation in hand

I was eating at an Indian restaurant as part of a group for which someone else had responsibility. During the process of ordering, one person said, 'Let's ask for a special deal before we order and try to get a good selection for £10 each.' The leader of the party was unsure. Essentially, he was uncomfortable with the suggestion, so a vague proposal was made, something like 'We would like 10 per cent discount, please.' There was no commitment in the request and the waiter said nothing. Nothing was agreed.

The approach was treated casually because that's exactly what it was. When the bill was presented at the end, there was no discount. When pressed, the waiter simply said that the manager was away and he had no authority to give a discount. The meal cost nearly £20 per head. It cost us all because there was no commitment to the negotiation. It was treated hopefully, casually, and therefore without authority.

Objective

Once the issue of commitment is settled, we must have clear objectives. Otherwise we will invariably settle for less than we need to. Not being sure of what we want is a common reason for getting poor negotiated results. Ask for more and you get more, ask for less and you get less. If you don't have clear objectives you won't know where to aim, and in every negotiation you will end up 'shooting from the hip'. This will always reduce your authority and will also leave you feeling less than confident. You will get less.

Objectives for your company

We need to establish clearly what our company objectives are, what business the company is in. This can cover many areas, but in the context of negotiation we need to have an overall objective that states our profit levels, the type of business or supply that we want, the type of product or service we want and the levels at which we want to buy and sell.

One legitimate objective would be for a business manager, an owner or a buyer to aim to reduce overall costs by 15 per cent while improving specific elements of supply. On the other hand, an owner or salesperson could have an objective of increasing the value of every sale by 10 per cent. By that I don't mean more sales, I mean better sales. More sales is also a good objective but it is not primarily a negotiation-related objective. The two could comfortably sit together.

Objectives for the negotiation in hand

Before we start negotiation we must know what our goals or objectives are. What is our ideal position, how can we support it or defend it? What are the objectives on price, on delivery, on volume, on frequency? What do we want to achieve from the other person? The clearer these objectives are, the more likely we are to ask for them and the more likely it is that we will get them. The more you ask for what you want, the more you will get.

Strategy

Strategy for the company

Once we have clear objectives for our company, we must then put a strategy in place. Our strategy is simply a series of pre-planned steps which enable us to realise those objectives. In other words, we know exactly what to do, when to do it and how, in order to achieve what we have set ourselves. In broad terms it will include:

- **defining which person or people are responsible for the negotiation process;**
- **training the person or people responsible for the negotiation process;**
- **planning for negotiation with existing long-term business relationships;**
- **putting times in the diary for review meetings with customers/suppliers.**

My good friend Nick Robinson – Honorary Chairman of the Marketing Guild – talks about the five-month itch and the nine-month itch in any long-term relationship. What he is referring to is the fact that there is bound to be dissatisfaction in any long-term relationship at particular points. The five-month itch occurs for a variety of reasons. Maybe the supplier has not quite met their deadlines. Maybe the buyer's aspirations have not been matched.

The supplier in this case should be defending their corner. They should stay in contact regularly. They should provide reams of paper showing results, reports, savings improvements. They should also stay close, visiting in person every two or three weeks. Around the nine-month point in any contractual relationship, the supplier should be aware that a good buyer is already considering other companies, prices are coming in and preliminary negotiations may well be taking place. Now is the time to romance your client like mad.

If you are the buyer in the relationship, you should be gathering information that will help in a review process, information that will help in the inevitable impending new negotiation phase.

Whether you are the buyer or supplier there is an opportunity here for you. Why not build in a quarterly review, which you drive? You set the agenda, you control the process. Call it a 'health check' and increase your negotiation power in the process.

Strategy for the particular negotiation in hand

Our objective for this particular negotiation must be crystal clear and we must know exactly how we intend to achieve it:

- **Who will conduct the negotiation for us?**
- **What information do we need about the other party and how will we secure it?**
- **What experts or specialists do we want to take?**
- **How do we ensure that we are controlling the whole process?**
- **Where should we hold the meeting?**
- **What do we need in print?**
- **What is our bottom line?**
- **What is our ideal win–win outcome?**

Tactics

Every negotiation has a tactical element. Every situation is different and how we read it will condition our success. Many tactics are provided in this book. Think through which ones are likely to be most effective. We need to know which tactics we want to use, which ones are favoured by us and which ones our opposite number is likely to be using. Before a particular negotiation, skim through these tactics. Jot down the ones that seem most appropriate, think through how you might use them, or how they might be used against you. Incidentally, in the process take note of the ones you enjoy and the ones that come most naturally to you, as invariably they will be the ones that work best for you.

Late one Friday night I spoke to a client who had a meeting with a potential buyer for his company on Monday. He wanted some guidelines, so we chatted through all the possible tactics he could use and which ones his counterpart might use. Within 10 minutes or so he was confident that he had the right approach. Those 10 minutes will have dramatically affected his performance on the Monday – time well spent.

Seven key elements

Remembering all the key elements in negotiation can be tricky and I find it useful to have a simple memory jog. To aid this process I use another acronym PREPBAR©. It's easy to recall and helps get every negotiation into focus and into the right sequence. The acronym works like this:

Plan and prepare
Rehearse
Explore and explain
Propose
Bargain
Agree
Review

Plan and prepare

If you negotiate casually you will never optimise your effectiveness. The more important the negotiation, the more preparation you should do. If you have not prepared properly and the other person has, you are at a disadvantage immediately. It will make you feel unprofessional and weak, and to be honest, at that moment, you are. Lack of preparation will nearly always cost you money.

When we prepare, we need to ask ourselves questions about the other person. We must form a judgement about what may or may not be important to that person:

- **What is important to them in making their decision?**
- **Where will they seek to negotiate?**
- **What combination of factors is likely to be important: cost, price, quantities, delivery, exclusive terms, credit, stock-holding, training, confidentiality, after-sales, maintenance, guarantees, contract length?**

Seek to uncover preferences, needs, obstacles, opportunities and problems. In each of these five cases, ask how they could be related to the negotiation in hand.

We also need to prepare our own position. What is our objective? What price level are we aiming for? Good negotiators have an ideal objective, which still enables a win–win outcome. They have also thought through a worst-case scenario, which is their bottom line, below which they will not go.

We must evaluate where we can shift in the process. We must ensure that we know the cost of everything and anything that we could use in the negotiation. Examples include the costs of giving on price, costs of changed payment, costs of rearranging delivery; in short, the cost of every proposed change you could make, or offer that you could give.

Having evaluated the information, effective negotiators plan their approach to trading and concessions. The effective negotiator will hunt out common ground and evaluate long-term needs, and as a result will have far more trading options.

Summarising our process of preparation – effective negotiation will depend on your accurately identifying at the preparation stage:

- **the other person's possible opening statement or position;**
- **how you will move from that opening statement towards your aspirations;**
- **your counterpart's potential problems, obstacles, opportunities, needs and preferences;**
- **your ideal and your bottom line;**
- **the cost of any possible movement you might make and its benefit to your counterpart;**
- **the concessions your counterpart could make and how you might make them appear trivial or worthless.**

I was working with one large European company doing some training for their teams of buyers. Each buyer had a supplier portfolio in excess of £15 million. During the consulting phase of the project we interviewed the buyers to ask how much time was spent on planning and preparation. Most had no real idea. It averaged out at a few hours per supplier; the most time any buyer spent was one half day.

I have worked both sides of the negotiating process hundreds of times. What struck me was that with their time pressures and other commitments, the longest period given was half of one day for preparation.

Let me share with you what I shared with these buying teams. Having run large companies as an MD and sold for other companies I can tell you that if your purchase with us was, say, 5 per cent of our sales, then we would spend one day on preparing and rehearsing a negotiation as an absolute minimum. We would spend more if we were not ready. How would we know if we were not ready? If we still had unanswered questions or if we had concerns that were not yet dealt with, we were clearly not ready.

If your spend with us was 40–50 per cent, then as the CEO, I would be personally involved, and with a team we might spend up to a week preparing for these negotiations. Often these moments were the biggest single moments in our business year.

Subsequently we did the negotiation planning sessions with these European teams and showed them what areas they might include in their planning. Then we asked them to calculate where they would get the necessary information and to calculate how much time they should diarise. The minimum now was three days and most of the team allocated four to five days. The results were measurable positively in the multi-millions.

Reader offer

We introduced these teams and countless other negotiators from small sole traders to multinational corporations to the planogram©. This is a copyright document that helps individuals identify the potential gaps in the planning and preparation phase of negotiation. For a free copy of the planogram please e-mail enquiries@insight-marketing.com and simply put Planogram in the subject line.

For extra tips on using social media to help you plan and prepare turn to Chapter 17.

Rehearse

Every major negotiation I have undertaken I have always rehearsed. It is a key to confidence. It is a key to uncovering likely and less likely potential problems and difficulties.

How do you rehearse? Write down your approach. Write down your key statements. Write down your response. What I do is to sit in my office and practise out loud. I will prepare visual material – OHP slides, PowerPoint or a simple flip-chart presentation. I will have every key point substantiated or affirmed with facts, figures, pie charts and statistics. I look at all that material with sceptical eyes to see how my approach could be countered or sunk! I make changes.

Try it! Tell yourself what you are going to say, how you will say it, where and in what order. Rehearse how your opposite number might do the same. Try to imagine all the possible responses and develop your counter moves.

Average negotiators will spend approximately the same time as good ones on the preparation phase. Effective negotiators, however, not only get the information but spend quality time rehearsing various applications of those facts until they are sure that they have the right approach.

I was working for a European client putting together a negotiation in London. We spent hours preparing, over the phone and by fax. We produced slides, OHPs and printed proposal documents. We checked every one and talked through potential weak spots. We were thoroughly prepared, but he was still willing to come to London hours early. We sat in the Grosvenor Hotel in Park Lane and rehearsed our individual roles again and again until we were both sure that we had it right. The outcome was superb, but it was no accident. It was down to hours of planned preparation, followed by hours of planned rehearsal.

A consultant acquaintance of mine was consulting for an international computer company. He spotted a significant growth opportunity for them and agreed with the sales team to enter into negotiations with the client. He was told by the sales team to meet in the client's car park 30 minutes beforehand, to run through their approach. He rightly challenged the arrangement but was told 'That's what we normally do'.

The consultant got held up by an accident en-route, and arrived in the car park at the start of the meeting. He ran in breathlessly and the receptionist escorted him to the meeting room. He went into the room, apologised for being late, and sat down next to what he thought were his colleagues only to be gently told by the client, 'I think you should be sat with your team rather than ours!'.

The story got worse. His colleagues began speaking on the topic he was expert on and the colleague then said to the consultant perhaps you would like to tell us about xyz. The consultant was totally unprepared on the newly introduced topic, and the whole negotiation moved from agreeing terms back to buying and selling, and the business was lost in its entirety. This was a significant entry project at around £1.5 million. The moral was very simple. The expertise was there, the negotiation skills were there, all the players had competence, the product was outstanding but lack of rehearsing on a major project cost dearly, and to my knowledge was never recovered.

Do it for each other. If you are in a buying team, how about scripting all the nasty things a supplier could do or could say and then plan your response and then rehearse how you would say it. You might even care to do some informal role plays together until you feel confident.

One of the things I would encourage you to consider in this context is to shadow learn or to find a mentor. I was part of a team recently running a two day event for 350 of the United Kingdom's top young leaders. One of my tasks was to provide a keynote speech on leadership. Whilst preparing I was celebrating my birthday with my family on our boat and found myself reflecting as one often does on a birthday.

I thought about the talk and thought if it was me sat there where they were sitting, what would I have found most helpful 20 years ago. I had the same thoughts whilst preparing for these two days. And if I had one key to a successful life, or one key to a successful career in negotiation I would say it has to be this one – find a mentor or at least find someone from whom you can shadow learn.

I can tell you now in buying or selling, no matter how experienced I thought I was, no matter how inexperienced I felt I was, I would find some of the best performers and if I could I would ask them to mentor me, or at least to let me rehearse my planned negotiation in front of them, and I would *carpe diem*, seize the day, with that opportunity.

Let me put it this way. If I was dropped into a war zone as a soldier, whether I was already well trained or a new recruit, I would not be looking for young gung-ho soldiers to teach me the ropes. I would be looking for someone with experience of serving in a conflict and they would be my source of shadow learning. What is shadow learning? It is letting someone else show you their way of doing it and wherever possible and wherever appropriate copying their method or their process.

Explore and explain

At some point, each side describes their position clearly. However, your goal should be to let your counterpart talk. Your job is to be in control. You can help yourself by having a written agenda that follows these key elements and puts you automatically in the driving seat. The simplest way to stay in control is to begin by asking questions. The buying and selling has already been done and you normally begin by asking the other party, 'Can we proceed with this as it stands?' In nearly every case the answer is a qualified 'No'. By the way, if they say 'Yes' immediately, it probably means you have undershot quite significantly in what you could have achieved.

But they say 'No'. You must then draw them out, get them to describe their position. The more you can get them to talk, the better. Try to keep quiet. Don't come back quickly with your own responses. Use positive phrases that will encourage them to keep talking. You might use phrases like 'I see' or 'Sure, I understand' and then follow it each time with a phrase like 'What else is important to you in this discussion?' followed by 'Does that cover all the issues from your point of view?'

Key note:
Create an agenda and let that help you control the process.

Propose

If they signal at this stage, you can respond. If they have no proposal of their own, it is your time to make a proposal. It does not hurt to allow the other party to propose their solution first. It will often cause them to give away concessions too early. It will give us a mirror into their mind, it will give us glimpses of what they are thinking. It will nearly always show up small cracks in their authority or power through which we can later drive the wedge of careful questions.

If the other party presents their position first, you have two choices. You can either accept their position and settle for less than you should. Or you can do what you must do, and that is to offer your counter-proposal.

In many cases their proposal and your response will not be enough to reach agreement. The likelihood is that there will still be a considerable distance between what they want and what you have counter-proposed. The next few words will make or break you, and those words have to be words that bargain.

Bargain

How do we bridge this very real gap, and move both of our interests towards a positive solution? Unskilled negotiators simply give, and the first place they give is price. It's the easy way out; it removes pressure for the moment but it will always cost you.

The only effective response here is for us to *trade* or *bargain*. The dictionary puts it this way: 'To *bargain* means to make it a condition of an agreement that something should be done.' If the other party wants us to move or concede on some of the terms and conditions, then bargaining by its very nature implies that we must get them to move on some of their terms and conditions. I cannot stress this enough, because every true negotiation goes through this bargaining phase. This is where your preparation pays off. You have thought through beforehand what you are willing to trade and you have thought through beforehand what you will ask them to trade. Every other approach is conceding, not negotiating. This is the pivotal point, this is where you become effective or mediocre. Get this bargaining phase right and you will secure advantage after advantage on every deal you make. Every other approach will without doubt cost you money.

Agree

It seems so obvious, but so many unskilled negotiators forget to confirm what is agreed. In the intensity of the bargaining process it is easy to forget what has actually been agreed. The objective of every negotiation is to reach agreement.

Remember, agreement does not just refer to the final conclusive signing of the deal. There are many points of agreement along the way. Both are important. At every point, wherever and whenever you can agree it is important to make the positive point of confirming that agreement.

Make a virtue of every point agreed. Take a bit of time and write it down. Let them know that is what you are doing and let them see you do it. Read it back to confirm it, and sound pleased. For both parties, en-route agreement is a positive feeling, in an intense environment.

When you reach what appears to be final agreement, summarise your understanding of the situation and write it down. Sometimes you can say, 'I will get this on the PC this afternoon; however, I have the key points written out here. Can we photocopy these and initial them before I leave?' If they say 'Yes', which is the normal response at this point, we have absolute clarity and agreement on the terms. If they hesitate, we can clear up any misunderstanding and ensure we reach agreement before we leave.

One of my clients selling computers had secured what he thought was an agreed deal with a major bank: an initial delivery worth in the region of £100k. The order form had been made up in the name of my client and had been verbally agreed by the bank, with the paperwork promised. My client represented two major PC manufacturers – international household names – and in good faith told the unsuccessful supplier that the deal was going to their competitor unless they could do something better.

The salesman went on holiday. When he came back the PC manufacturer had gone in with slightly used models and had secured the deal unethically. Agreement should have been more firm; he thought he had the deal. In reality it was not as clear-cut as he imagined it to be. He should have made certain that agreement was unequivocally in place.

Review

At the end of each significant negotiation we take some minutes to assess our performance and take note of successes and areas where we perceive weakness.

Target & actual cost price increase (CPI) or cost price reduction (CPR).
Target and actual terms.
Impact on any category targets.
On each of the 7 steps (PREPBAR©).

- **What went well?**
- **What didn't?**
- **What did I try for the first time?**
- **What could I have done better?**
- **Where did I feel vulnerable and unprepared?**
- **What personal development action do I need to take?**
- **What needs to be in writing?**
- **What action or follow up is needed?**

4

Introductory comments

The quandary of uncertainty

Negotiation is inherent in human nature and with it a sense of uncertainty. That's one of the reasons why some people dislike the process. Many of us would far rather prices, proposals and terms were fixed in every way, so that we could ask for what we want, and make a decision based purely on our perception of value. What causes this quandary?

Simply, the fact that everything is unknown. I don't know what a 'good' deal is in this case. Is the other person ripping me off? What will my peers, my family, my boss think of the agreement I have reached? Could I have got a better deal in some way? All this produces stress, unease, uncertainty.

Some years back, the British government faced this quandary of uncertainty with BSE or mad cow disease and subsequently foot and mouth disease. In both cases they didn't know whether to cull thousands or millions of cattle. They didn't know how much the European Union would cough up in compensation for culling or how much they would have to ask the British taxpayer for. For that reason, in both cases they found it difficult to decide where to start in their negotiating process. And the politicians' stumbling, rambling political performance on television revealed that fact starkly.

The same can happen to any one of us reading this material. In many cases we really do not know what price to start at. Many times we will not know for sure whether we could have got more. We may never know whether we could have persuaded our counterpart to move further. That is the reality of many of the negotiations we are involved with.

My daughter has just purchased her first home here in the UK. The asking price was £115,000 we offered £98,000 and finally settled on £108,000. The negotiation was robust and the reality is twofold; first she has a house she likes and represents good value but second we will never know, could we have got the house for less? That's the quandary of uncertainty. The upside is that the reality is also clear, if we hadn't negotiated we would have paid £7,000 or 6.6 per cent more than we finally paid.

Avoid intransigence

The easy way out is an offer or price from which we refuse to budge. It removes the indecision. It removes the risk of causing offence. It removes the risk of getting it wrong.

However, we should always expect a competent business person to offer less than we ask for. Putting it another way, it is very rare in my experience for a potential customer to say, 'This is fantastic, please let me pay more than you are asking.'

I have four children and I know that negotiation is a natural part of their behaviour. As they grew up we would often give extra chores, for which they would get an increase in pocket money. I remember one turning point in my son's business development. On one occasion he came back and said, 'This money is not enough for the extra work.' The trouble was that we had become dependent on his work. And he was doing a very good job. Now I could have been intransigent and made a decision from which I refused to budge. But if I had done that, what would the outcome have been? Think it through with me – I would have lost his willing cooperation. So negotiation was inevitable.

Over many years I have been responsible for purchasing cars appropriate to our image in the market. Two makes suited our requirements: Volvo and BMW. For years BMW dealers would take a stance of intransigence from which they would not shift. In other words, they would not negotiate. In every case I bought Volvo because BMW would not negotiate on price, service or extras. Last year BMW did begin to negotiate and they got my business for the first time in seven years; they could have had it much sooner by avoiding intransigence.

One of my friends was finance director for a major international distribution company. They conducted a sales presentation, which they won, for distribution services with a national chain. Before the contract was ratified the national chain was subject to a take-over and the new parent simply renewed the contract with the existing supplier.

The following year both companies were pitched against each other. My friend's company was in many ways the better choice and probably the preferred supplier. They were asked to review their set-up costs. These included items such as training and software implementation – fairly soft costs. But company policy was essentially intransigent. They simply would not budge on those costs. The other supplier offered them totally free and got the business.

To the casual observer it may appear that price was the issue. The reality was that intransigence was the issue. When my friend evaluated the cost of the set-up compared with the net profit over even the first year the difference was minuscule.

My friend put it this way: 'Being obsessed with short-term profitability led us to miss the whole deal. It stopped us from seeing the supplier's point of view and wasted enormous amounts of time spent in preparation and presentation.' Intransigence may remove some uncertainty. But it will always cost us.

Understand aspiration

Most companies that go bankrupt, as we well know, are usually busy. They were just busy doing the wrong things, but more importantly, on the *wrong terms*. The competitive free market economy puts a downward pressure on our aspirations.

Human nature and the free market economy also inspire positive aspiration. The combination affects what we aim for, what we expect to get and what we would ideally like to achieve. Skilled buyers understand this and will use a routine tactic. When we give our price, these buyers rarely say, 'Fantastic, how reasonable!' No! They say, 'What? How much?' When they do that, or when they tell us that our competitors' prices are much lower, what is the impact? Their technique forces us to lower our aspirations. We tend to lower them, and lower our price.

The reverse should be true. For that reason, negotiation is not for the few, it is for every responsible businessman or woman. Every one of us wanting to achieve increased profit will need to face negotiation with a brave heart and a sound approach. Our first response, buyer or seller, is to defend our aspiration consistently.

Never say yes first time

Of all the principles we shall look at, this one is the simplest and probably the most effective. *Remembering this will save you money and increase your profit on every single deal you make.*

This principle should be a reflex action. I was co-presenting at a seminar in a large room at Heathrow. One of the other presenters asked the delegates this question: 'How many of you here never pay the full rate for hotel rooms?' About one-third of the room raised their hands. That means that two-thirds were regularly paying too much for overnight stays.

A friend of mine was staying away in a hotel to prepare for a new seminar he was writing. The hotel was one of a nationally recognised and reputable chain, located in Milton Keynes. He simply asked, 'What is your best rate?' and managed to negotiate from an offered rate of £120 down to £78 per night. Never say yes first time.

What about when you buy advertising? Did you know that you should never pay the full rate? Agencies usually claim 10 per cent, and you can use that fact to get 10 per cent reduction straight away. Call some advertisers to see what response they have achieved, and use that information to lower the magazine's aspiration. You can even send a cheque for half the rate, and say, 'Feel free to cash my cheque when you place my advert on the inside back cover.'

What we think conditions our approach

The other party in a negotiation often exercises more authority, not because they have it in reality, but simply because they *think* they have it. We can make this worse by allowing ourselves to believe that our counterpart has more strength than they have. When we do that, we compound the strength they already feel.

Your counterpart, whoever they are, can appear more powerful. Maybe because you feel insecure. Perhaps because they have the ability to pay you or supply something you badly need. The reality is often the reverse: they need what you can offer, the problems you can overcome, the opportunities you can create, the obstacles you can remove, the preferences you can satisfy.

We must build and enhance our authority in negotiation. How you see it determines your outcome. The old adage 'Seeing is believing' applies here. Authority and confidence stem from our own perception. The authority you carry in a negotiation is largely based on your confidence. It is a reflection of your state of mind but it is real and has real effect on the outcome.

Confidence is a key. If you lose your own confidence, the counterpart will intuitively pick that up, and you will end the negotiation in a much weaker position than you need to. Tactics therefore need to be clear before you go into the negotiation. If your counterpart perceives a loss of confidence, you won't regain the high ground.

Authority comes from confidence. Our sources of confidence come from the preparation phase: thinking through all the advantages we have to offer, thinking through all the gaps in the weaknesses of the other party. We strengthen our mind and strengthen our position. To aid us in this process we need to assess and build our authority.

Before presenting a solution, make sure you understand the needs

Every prospect has different problems, different requirements, different needs. We must spend time asking questions, probing, exploring and then matching the correct solution.

One of the common mistakes made is to ask questions in a hurry, identify one need and then assume that is the real problem. In negotiation we must make sure we understand before we present our solution. Even if a prospect states, 'This is the solution that I want', do not accept that conclusion at face value. Instead, say, 'Certainly – can I ask what it is precisely that you want to achieve?'

It may well be that there is a different solution or one that only your company can offer, so when presented with a prospect's own solution as a *fait accompli* always ask questions back to ascertain how best to serve them.

Build value before presenting your solution

A common mistake is offering your solution too early. Offering premature solutions to half-developed desires or inadequately assessed needs will produce objections. We must learn to build value in the prospect's mind. If you or your salespeople are regularly getting lots of objections, you can be fairly certain that you are not building value adequately.

I was on the phone to a company called Intone Designs. We supplied them with a 12-month service, essentially providing them with sales leads for kitchen units, which they supply and fit. I was endeavouring to achieve a negotiation for renewal for another 12 months. He said, 'I don't think we will go ahead; it's not been working for us'. I found myself asking how he had been using the service and gave him my normal stock answers. I told him how he could improve performance over 14 times using a method we ourselves were using every day. I was at the point of pressing for the renewal, but I was aware that this was not scratching him where it itched!

So I started asking him other questions, 'Tell me about your company, what new things are you doing?' He began to describe a new concept – commercial quality kitchens for installation in elderly and sheltered housing. He was suddenly animated and motivated. Instead of talking about renewal we talked about all the new sales leads in his geographical area for elderly persons' homes and sheltered housing – he was eager to take another 12 months of the leads service. Why? Because we had uncovered the value that this would give him, in particular with his new ideas of fresh markets for his kitchens.

Enhance your authority

The authority of print

There is a real authority in having prices, costs and details in print. Printed material carries an inherent believability. If you are a buyer, you may choose to have target prices, or competitive prices, or last year's prices. You may have a printed page detailing the implications of proposed prices and their impact on profit, on staffing levels, etc. You may even have a summary business plan built on your ability to achieve a given price for this contract. It is so simple but so effective it intimidates the seller into a defensive posture.

For consultants or others selling professional services, what often happens, for example, is that you quote a daily fee of £200 or £2,000 and the buyer has nothing to measure it against. How do they know that this is in fact a reasonable rate? How do they know that you haven't made this figure up? How do they know that you are not just 'trying it on'? Having it in print will make it appear credible, more believable and more legitimate.

Either side of the negotiating table, having printed material disarms the other person. It makes it more difficult for them to squeeze more out of the deal. Printed price lists, letters from superiors, letters from current customers or suppliers, departmental budgets, letters from your superior, standard forms, articles from newspapers, competitors' brochures – all these have the power of authority for you to use. Just yesterday a national lettings agency sent me the printed document for a lettings agreement. For one level of service it stated 16 per cent. It was *in print*. I rang the manager and challenged the assumption, and immediately got a lower rate of commission agreed. But I noticed with interest my own inner reluctance to make that call. Why? Because there was an authority simply gained by having a higher figure in print. For some this can be achieved by having prices on your website.

Incidentally, if you don't have any material pre-printed then at the very least produce it on your own word processor with a date and a reference to give it validity.

Whatever printed material you deem appropriate in a particular negotiation, use it to validate your limited ability to move from a desired position. It makes it harder for the other person to ask you for any form of concession and it will build your confidence for the position you are taking. If the tactic is being used on you, one response is to say, '*Actually, that is not relevant to this particular application.*' It doesn't always work but it does buy you some time!

Ed is a shy person and a computer guru. He was telling me how he went to a high street outlet and bought a joystick. The joysticks were on sale for £80; he saw a slightly damaged unit and bargained for it at £65. When he tried it out, it was faulty, so he took it back and asked for cash back, and a receipt clearly marked with the model on it. They had no others in stock, so he went to another store where the unit was on sale for £90. He produced his receipt for £65, and asked them if they could match the price, which they did. His printed receipt was a source of authority.

I got an e-mail from a business owner who had purchased this book at the airport en-route to an important negotiation. The concept of preparation, rehearsal and print impacted on him on the plane so on arrival he woke early in his hotel and sent me an e-mail as follows:

> The preparation I had done on the plane and completed at 6 am was inadequate but a lot better than nothing. I felt I had gained experience and confidence as I had practised a range of tactics through my night-time adventures. I printed off the documents I had quickly prepared to back up my proposal along with a nice formal agenda and went for it! The result? Fantastic.

Simple really, plan, prepare and get your critical materials in print.

The authority of information

Here we must take the time and make the effort to collect as much information as we can about the other side and their organisation.

'W' questions are the method: what, which, when, why, who and how? Too often, busy professional people talk rather than listen. The classic example is when you get an enquiry, on an incoming telephone call. The prospect has found your name in a directory. Let's say he calls and says, 'Can you tell me about your training facilities?'

We answer that we've got ropes, we've got camping facilities, we've got safety certification, we've got brilliant instructors, we've got acres of land, we've got, we've got, we've got! What we've actually got is no power, no negotiation strength and no real perception of his requirements. And worst of all, we have given him a load of information about ourselves and further weakened our position.

When he says, 'Can you tell me about your training facilities?', the reply should be 'Certainly, my name is... – who am I speaking to? And your company name? To enable me to get back to you, may I have your telephone number? Before I tell you, could I ask you...?' And then we move into our power-enriching W questions:

- **What are you looking to achieve from your training?**
- **How have you used outdoor training before?**
- **How many participants?**
- **What previous training have they had?**
- **What are their responsibilities in the company or the team?**
- **What particularly are you looking for in the successful provider?**
- **What difficulties have you experienced with previous suppliers?**

That is the key question. It will often expose real need or weakness and will give you a significant point of authority. In fact it's an easy question to remember, any time you want to prise out some important information, it often goes to the heart of some difficulty or pain in our counterpart's world.

Stay in tight control of the flow of information to the other party about *your* organisation. Take great care in exposing *your* needs, *your* dependency, staff shortages, cost breakdowns. The only information we should give the other party is the advantage, the gain, the benefit. Which is why we must ask the W questions.

W questions enable us to uncover what the other person really *needs and wants*. If we are selling, they enable us to discover with accuracy which unique selling point (USP) is relevant, meaningful and powerful. If you think you have a 'cure-all' USP, but in reality it is not meaningful or relevant to this buyer, it is clearly not a unique perceived benefit at all.

Whether you are buying or selling, you have the freedom to be silent. Don't be under pressure to answer every question. You don't have to talk. Often, if you don't respond to the other person's comment or question, he will speak after a short, sometimes uncomfortable wait. In that situation your counterpart may give away more information – information that he intended to keep from you. Don't be unduly concerned by apparently embarrassing silences.

Because of your silence you will learn more and more, which is to your advantage in the negotiation. Also, remaining silent for a while gives you more time to think, more time to decide on your next move.

The authority of patience

Rush equals loss. There is often pressure to agree a deal, to close the sale or make the purchase. The tyranny of the urgent shouts so loudly that we don't give time to uncover information.

Some time back, I received a call from an electronics company wanting what they said was a marketing review. I was under pressure from a heavy workload. I told them I don't do speculative visits. I made some assumptions from a rushed conversation about what they were really looking for. I then put together a proposal, equally rushed, and made a subsequent follow-up call.

During the follow-up call it became clear that my rush had resulted in three damaging things. First, I had obtained inadequate information about them and their requirements. Second, I voluntarily printed a cost breakdown, which I shouldn't have done and from which they immediately negotiated. Third, my overall proposal was weak because I had not focused on the key points. I had totally missed the USP and was then on an uphill struggle to regain my lost ground. All that because I was in too much of a hurry.

What about time pressures on the buyer? When you are buying, you can usually build in time to allow you to negotiate from maximum strength. The longer you can keep the salesperson waiting for an answer, the more likely he or she is to concede, to give things away that he or she would not otherwise have given. The more relaxed you are about the buying process, the more pressure it exerts on the seller.

Bide your time and wait for that moment where your counterpart expresses weakness. Wait until your opposite number is vulnerable, look for that moment and then move in.

One of my clients has a specialist skill in the buying and

selling of businesses. The key, he told me, lies in timing. Knowing the right time is the critical factor in both buying and selling. There are all kinds of reasons why individuals might sell their company. They might be near retiring age with no family to pass the business on to. The business may need to move on, and they may not have the resource or the infrastructure to do it. But even when these needs are clear, you have to wait and be patient.

I have watched it myself, particularly with sole traders; you negotiate and think the time is right but they pull back at the last minute. Not as a tactic, simply out of uncertainty. If you try to pressurise them, you nearly always frighten them off. Patience is what you need. Sometimes it can take years. You may come close to agreement several times, with the uncertain party backing off several times. It is normal, and if you want to succeed you must prepare yourself for this inevitable delay.

The party who is most compelled by time is weaker – plan to have time, build in time.

The authority of positive posturing

All the pressures on us, both buyer and seller, are downward as far as price is concerned. We need to stop the rot and build value, build authority, build confidence.

This is not mind over matter. This is stark reality. For sellers, your own thoughts and the negative environment that so often surrounds you mean that you go into negotiation already feeling that your prices are too high. In fact it is amusingly uncommon to meet salespeople who believe their prices are low or right. Any buyer worth his or her salt is going to try to make you feel that even more keenly.

One of the things that can be hard for salespeople is that in nearly every application more people say 'No' than 'Yes'. There is nothing wrong with that. Good salespeople may secure one sale in every three to four appointments. They should be proud of that achievement. However, their mind has been told 'No' more than 'Yes'. Let's say they do 100 appointments per month. That means 75 people or companies have said 'No' and only 25 have said 'Yes'. As a sales manager I would probably be pleased with that performance, and rightly so. But what of the effect on the salespeople's state of mind? I was listening to a sales trainer recently in Canada who insisted that all his salespeople had 20 'No's per week – otherwise they didn't get paid! That is positive posturing towards the 'No's.

Whatever our job, it can condition us to go into negotiation in a negative frame of mind. Working environments often bring us into contact with criticism and complaints. If we hear negative things often enough we can begin to believe them. These negative inputs can weigh us down. If we are not careful, our motivation and determination can drown under their weight.

Skilled negotiators spend time building up their own confidence, making sure before any significant negotiation that they feel good about the process and their role in it, objectively restating to themselves the positive value of this deal, this agreement, and their impact upon it. It often helps to write down key positive statements about the project, the product, the deal and its effect. Doing this is cathartic; it begins to wash clean those negative stains and provides a clean fresh edge to our motivation and performance.

The authority of levers

We have been taught that the primary lever in the negotiation is your USP, which we have already looked at in some detail: your product or service, the company, you the person. In 20 years of negotiation, the USP has always been proposed as the primary key for increased profit, better deals and greater profit: the primary key to increasing power and increasing confidence. If we don't have USPs, or are unclear about them, our power is fundamentally weakened.

The unique selling proposition does, however, have a major drawback and I wonder if you can think what it is? Let me put it another way. When you read the words 'unique selling proposition', who are they usually referring to? You, the seller – and actually that is the cardinal sin of marketing. So what do we do? We develop the USP into what we call in my organisation the MDSA© (Measurable Difference & Specific Advantage). Now that is about your counterpart and measures the specific advantage to them, in units that are tangible for them. The clearer that measurable difference and the more specific the advantage, the more authority you have.

Distance is another lever. Distance retains strength: if we are weaker, meet them, if we are stronger, don't meet them. I was tying up a deal with an international author and seminar presenter. I had quoted £5,200 for a particular package and I was sent a message by his office manager (via his car phone) saying the deal could go ahead if we could agree £5,000. He was a buyer with significant strength and he retained it by using the distance. I couldn't contact him personally and he used that fact cleverly.

The third lever is 'fallback'. Fallback means that I have a good or acceptable alternative to agreement being negotiated. The more easily we can walk away from the negotiating environment, the better our result.

If you need the deal more than you can cope with losing it, you will be less authoritative in the negotiation. If there is real pressure on you to secure this one at all costs, it will affect the outcome negatively, particularly if you believe there is little pressure on your counterpart to do the same.

The authority of resolved weaknesses

In nearly every negotiation both parties have concealed areas of weakness. If our counterpart is effective, they will hunt these areas out and exploit them. So they should! How can they do that with such apparent ease? If we don't deal with our areas of exposure or weakness, they will sense uncertainty and chase it until the weakness is exposed. They will then rightly use that to strengthen their own position. Our own attention is then focused inevitably on the exposed weakness and we are left in a defensive state trying to limit whatever damage is now being done.

The answer lay with us all along. The fact is, we probably knew the weakness existed and even if our counterpart had not raised it, it was busy undermining our confidence and eroding our authority.

The way to handle this is to put some time aside, and list all the elements of your business that are relevant to any negotiation. In one column detail all the strengths; in another, list any weaknesses you can think of. Simply thinking through those weaknesses and listing them, facing them head on, can be of great value. That process on its own can often yield some obvious answers. It may even solve some niggling business problems for you. But the real goal is to turn them into positive attributes or strengths. At the very least, be totally confident in your own ability to deal with any purported weakness in the negotiation. Be confident in your own method of handling it in the process.

The authority of clear internal relationships

This may seem a little strange but in most settings you are not negotiating in a vacuum. Your category manager, or senior buyer, or your colleagues have certain aspirations and expectations and so does your director. Have you sat down and chatted through their place in the process? Are there specific negotiations where you might like to ask them in as an expert or as an authority where it would help that negotiation?

You need to establish for yourself if it's not clear, what areas they might want to be involved in. It could be as simple as 'John, here are the four key negotiations I have coming up, are there any areas you would like to be personally involved in or is there any posturing you would like to give to me on this one?'

Sometimes it will happen that you work hard to secure a deal and one of your internal managers takes the credit for that – ah well such is life!

If you have to report back to a superior – and let's assume there is a strong likelihood that you will not achieve the targeted terms for that supplier – don't just go to your superior with the bad news. Go with the issues yes, but go with your plan for moving forward so it is clear you have taken responsibility and given it thinking time to come up with your best solution. Show them your planning and preparation. Show them the tools you have used and show them your planned remedy or range of options. Then share it with them in that context looking for additional ideas and pointers.

6

Tactics and countermeasures

In any negotiation, tactics are regularly brought into play. It is vital that we know the most common ones. It is equally vital that we know how to counter if they are used on us in the process. If we are in buying mode, we can try these tactics or some variant of them. If we are in selling mode, we can learn ways to respond appropriately when these tactics are used on us, as they invariably will be.

Knowing and therefore identifying any tactic takes the emotion out of the system. It frees your mind to think about the countermeasures – ways to deal efficiently with the tactic. These tactics often appear as non-negotiable issues but in fact rarely are!

Aspiration lowering

How does the other person attempt to lower our aspirations on price? There are two commonly applied tactics. The first is to compare your offer with your competitors' terms or product. The second is a straightforward request.

Comparing your offer

Cost	They are cheaper.
Delivery	They can do the audit 10 days sooner.
Quantity	They are providing sample letters, adverts and telesales scripts.
New features	They provide a 60-day helpline.
Security	They guarantee our taxation liability, they guarantee safety.
Payment	They allow 90 days for payment.

Straightforward request

Here the other person may use a tricky phrase: 'At this point it is our company policy to agree suppliers' discount level' or 'It is normal business practice in these cases to agree supplier discount.'

Price is a legitimate and obvious target in any negotiation and every sensible buyer should try it. The phrase '*It is normal business practice*' is clever; it can easily catch you out. It can subtly put pressure on you to conform to what is being declared as normal. We should never succumb to the pressure to drop our price.

The first line of counter-attack is to ask '*Why?*' You can put it in a statement like this: 'You are suggesting that our price is too high. Can I ask too high in relation to what?'

What is the reason for asking a question like that? Simply that our counterpart's attempt to rot our price could mean any one of these:

- **It's more expensive than I thought.**
- **I want a discount.**
- **This is more than I can sanction.**
- **Somebody else is cheaper.**
- **I am not yet convinced of the value.**
- **This is actually outside our budget.**

Understanding the real reason behind the challenge to our price enables us to respond appropriately. We then trade; in other words, *nothing at all is ever given away*. Any ultimate adjustment in price must always be exchanged for something else from our counterpart.

A pre-emptive countermeasure to this tactic is to ask for more in the first place. Buyer or seller – ask for more, you get more. Aiming higher gives us room to negotiate. It means giving ourselves more room to make concessions; it means that we don't keep eroding company margins. The price, however, must be realistic and perceived to be legitimate. We can expect our counterpart to challenge anything that looks artificially high – we must have good reasons. If they think we are trying it on, they will have a cynical view of the rest of our negotiations that will prove most unhelpful, and jeopardise future business.

A further practical countermeasure is to stop, then slowly and deliberately use a calculator to see the real costs of conceding to price challenges. Let your opponent see you using it, too. Multiply by the number of clients, number of days per year, so that both you and they see the real impact of any concession. It also shows that you have done your homework and that you have legitimate reasons for defending that price.

It's all I have got

Your house is ideally situated and my wife and I like the area, but you want £250,000 and with our deposit and the maximum we can borrow, the most we can find is £240,000 – it's all I've got.

The implication is a positive attitude towards us and our proposal but an implied limit to the funds available.

A normal but wrong response is to offer discount. A good negotiator must have another proposal available. Any change to price must mean a change to the terms. If we are required to change the price, we must insist that they accept changes to the proposal or elements of it.

Suggesting a changed proposal will test whether our counterpart has genuinely limited funds. If they are not interested, they are simply trying it on. We might test the tactic by saying, 'Fine, can I assume that if we could arrange the mortgage through our contacts we can go ahead?'

The simple countermeasure in general terms to this tactic is to offer an alternative:

- **Offer changed methods of payment.**
- **Offer a change to the service – for example, instead of two days we could redesign the course into one longer day.**
- **Offer to change the whole package in some way – for example, the helpline, the printed report, the briefing session conducted by telephone rather than by visit, etc.**
- **Offer changed volumes, or changed delivery dates.**

The key is that *any change on price must accompany change in the proposal*, otherwise we give away what we should never give away.

I mentioned earlier how one of my recent clients used his strength by keeping his distance, and dealing with me through his office manager. You recall he was asking me to reduce my proposal by £200. I was frustrated, I was busy, I was tired and someone was lowering my aspirations. It would be so easy to rationalise away £200. But £200 × 10 clients per month × 10 months is £20,000. That is a lot of money. So I changed the proposal. I said we would agree to £5,000 but it meant reducing the number of hours available on the telephone helpline and we required payment on the day. A different price required a different proposal and we both settled happily for that.

The hurdle!

Countless times I have been in a negotiation and the other person has said, 'You must be joking' or 'You will have to improve that'.

They might say, 'You are getting close – *but*!' That, by the way, always means 'Your price is high and it's a *hurdle* to the agreement. Drop the hurdle and let's see what we can do.'

They are implying that price is the key issue and other elements of the negotiation are acceptable. Turn it to your advantage. Your immediate response should be something like this: 'From what you are saying, it seems that you are happy with the proposal. If we can agree together on price, can I assume we have a deal?'

What we are doing here is using the other person's ploy to our advantage, narrowing down any possible further areas of potential disagreement. Don't catch price rot! Performance is part of our price and we must communicate that. A carefully crafted approach would go like this: 'Let me ask you, isn't it true that all companies have a choice to make? They can either provide a service which does as much as possible for their customers, or they can provide a service which does just enough to get by with. Isn't that the choice that every company must make?' The other person usually says, 'Yes'. We say, 'Well, what would you prefer from us, as much as possible or just enough to get by with?'

We can do better on price *if you* accept the following. If we have to trade, we do so reluctantly. We make sure that any movement on our side is accompanied by movement on their side.

The A-Team factor

When my two sons were younger, our favourite joint viewing was *The A-Team*. One speciality would be when a hapless victim was interrogated by 'Mr T', a big and frightening individual, together with 'Face', who was always 'Mr Nice'. Mr T would always scowl, growl, threaten and bully. Face would then come and gently, quietly, offer a way out, 'If only you would talk'. He would offer a drink, offer kindness, offer much nicer-sounding alternatives. Nearly every time the victim would be conned. He would give in unnecessarily. In *Inspector Morse* you can see Morse and Lewis playing exactly the same roles.

The same tactic is applied in negotiation. The buyer brings in his financial director, who sourly pulls your proposal to pieces. She gets angry about your prices and may even raise her voice to you. After a while she gets called into another meeting.

The buyer turns round to you like an old friend. He apologises for his director and offers much more reasonable-sounding terms. That is danger time! Beware of his tactic, because it seems so reasonable, but only in comparison with the bully. The bully has set us up for Mr Nice, who then seems reasonable. The problem is that because we have been deflated and our aspirations have been lowered we can too quickly negotiate from the wrong base.

The best possible thing you can do is laugh when you spot the tactic. Lower their authority by showing them you know what they are doing. Then don't negotiate immediately, otherwise you will be comparing the reasonable buyer's demands with the bully. Instead, excuse yourself, give yourself time, take a loo break and take time to compare current demands with what you had already determined as your negotiating position.

Erosion

My family and I visited a famous model village on the Isle of Wight. It was situated on a cliff top – right on the edge – with spectacular views over the Atlantic Ocean. A few days after we visited the place, it shut down because erosion from the constant pounding of the sea had eaten away at its foundations. Some of the exhibits had slipped into the sea – lost for ever. Erosion is often not taken seriously. In negotiation we can make it work well for us.

Our counterpart has fixed terms or amounts or fixed prices. We keep eroding away at the edges, trying to make their firm stance give way. This is a marvellously effective tactic, which I try to use as routinely as I can. It works by using a simple question, 'If I buy this, will you throw in that?' I was buying some suits recently. I let it be known that I was interested in buying one suit. I asked, 'If I buy three, what discount will you give and how many shirts and ties will you throw in?' Whenever you are in buying mode, try to use this tactic. You can have some fun. Recently my two daughters went together to buy a new mobile phone each. They used the power of 'two purchases in one' to ask for more. 'I'm interested in this model. If I buy two, what is your best price and what else can you throw in?' The final erosion used this book. Carleen said, 'My dad has written a book on negotiation and if I don't go back with more than this I'm in trouble!' And on this occasion the girls got a great deal with a lot of fun in the process. Their buying tactic in this case was erosion.

If you are selling, beware because the buyer wants to get some little extras. These are dangerous because they often appear small, but multiplied they have a profound effect. We must price them, identify their real cost and be seen to be doing it. We must never give in to the eroding tactic. We must trade, not give in.

Let's say we are in property or estate agency. We offer to sell a house for 2.5 per cent commission. The owner wants to negotiate to 2 per cent. The value of the house is £200,000. Half a per cent. Doesn't sound very much, does it? In reality it is a great deal. Two per cent is £4,000; 2.5 per cent is £5,000. It means I am losing 20 per cent of my income and probably a much higher percentage of profit. If I make five similar sales each month, I am losing £5,000 per month or £60,000 per year.

Look at it in another light. If five houses per month at 2.5 per cent yields £80,000 profit each year, then that half per cent will reduce my profit from £80,000 to just £20,000. That half per cent has reduced my profit by a staggering 75 per cent.

I am often asked for training manuals. Say a buyer asks me for 100 extra training manuals – gently eroding my determination! I calculate how much that costs, possibly £5 each, and say incredulously, 'You are asking me to give away £500. I do five of these events each month and you are suggesting I give away £2,500 each month, that's £30,000 each year!'

It's calculator time again. Get out the calculator, let them see you do the sums, talk out loud while you do it, and make sure that the outcome is spoken out – and, ideally, written down – in front of the other party. It helps to let the other person see your calculations and your cost implications. Let them see on paper the calculation you have just made.

I will never forget the gasp in the training room. My colleague and I had just been training on erosion, and we asked the delegates in their teams to calculate the impact to their company, of 'just half a per cent'. They spent time in their teams calculating the impact on each person's individual negotiation, and then adding up to give the facilitator the team total. As I stood around the flip chart that day I could not believe my eyes. The total cumulative impact of the just half a per cent was £21 million. That is bottom line £21 million. The teams were stunned and the lesson was drilled in. Erosion is subtle but potent. Don't give into it.

The upward spiral

Have you ever climbed the spiral stairs of a lighthouse or some other tall building? I remember doing this with my children on several occasions. You think you are there, and then someone tells you there is more to climb! Unless you are really motivated, that extra upward effort can prove too much and you succumb to the downward pressure of gravity and your clinging children. The upward spiral in negotiation feels similar. You are sure you have reached the end and then your counterpart seems to have started all over again. It is very wearing and that is its danger.

This can be used by both buyer and seller. We may have got close to agreement in principle but then the other person lets time pass to lower our aspirations and does not send in the signed order form or does not ratify the agreement and then finds some way of starting the negotiation all over again.

I have seen this happen time and time again with salespeople. A salesman makes a sale and thinks he has agreed the terms. He tells his sales manager that they have a verbal agreement and they count it in the current month's sales figures. A few days before the end of the month the signed order form has not appeared. Suddenly now the sales manager is faced with a dilemma. He just has to have that business, because he has committed himself to the month's result. When he calls the prospective customer, the urgency will be clearly audible in his approach. The buyer will see the date, put two and two together and press for a better deal. In nearly every case the salesman or his manager will end up giving too much away.

As a means of using the upward spiral, it is a useful tactic for buyers to probe to find out from the salesman what pressures are on him or his company to meet monthly or quarterly figures. Ask the seller how his commission scheme operates, ask what figures are important to his company this month or this quarter. I used this tactic for one of my clients. I was negotiating on their behalf for some office equipment. We had secured some good deals but were unhappy with the proposal on fax machines. My client sends and receives over 100,000 faxes each year and we needed some robust, fast machines with specific functions. We approached the key suppliers, found some appropriate models and began to negotiate.

I knew which model we wanted, but could not achieve my target price. I did not want to pay for at least three months and my client could wait for delivery. The salesman had convinced himself he had the sale in the bag, so I stalled. I began asking the salesman about his own development within the company, his career, his commission.

From those questions I discovered that within one month he would be moving to another department. He needed to surpass a threshold figure, after which any sales brought in this month would be allowable as part of the commission scheme for his new job. My purchase could help him achieve that threshold.

I suggested that he take my proposal back to head office. My proposal was to buy at my target price. I would place the order now, and give him three post-dated cheques on the spot. He came back one day later and the deal was agreed.

Another variation is where buyer or seller may use the upward spiral by passing the final decision, or 'written approval', further and further up the management scale. In other words, they make it appear that they are not authorised to agree these 'additional points' – it must be referred to their superior. By inference, if we will drop these new requests or proposed changes they can still make the agreement. Call their bluff. They may be just as unwilling to start again as we are. You might start closing up your briefcase and say, 'I am sorry if we can't approve what I thought we had agreed. It may be that my MD will have to start discussions again with your boss.' It is usually enough; it is phrased in such a way that he can backtrack without losing face.

Upward spiral after agreement does sometimes happen even though it is unethical. I had a variation of this dirty trick played on me some time back. I was out with my family and some friends taking a walk in the New Forest. We stopped for afternoon tea in a tea-room and placed our order. We ordered tea to drink for four, three sodas and then asked for five scones with cream and jam. The proprietor said rather quickly, 'You want five cream teas', and we nodded assent without thinking.

You can guess the rest! The five cream teas included vast quantities of scones plus cakes, which we had not asked for. The price was of course far higher than the cost of five scones with cream and jam. It left a nasty taste in our mouths, not because we would have minded the proprietor trying to up-sell our order, but because it had been done in an underhand manner. The terms had been escalated unethically.

Sometimes if buyers do that to us, we can call their bluff again by saying that we will no longer do it for the original price and give them a new one. Then they have to negotiate all over again and may well be content to settle at the original price.

A friend of mine, Chris, was a skipper on one of the fishing boats that ply their trade in Poole, Dorset. He often feeds me with great anecdotes, and when he told me about 'Pirate George' I immediately thought of escalation.

Pirate George was an interesting and shrewd character. One evening Pirate George brought his boat close to Chris and said, 'Come with me we are going to make some money'. Close to Poole Town Quay, a 40ft ketch had caught its keel on a sand bar and had come to an abrupt halt. The boat had begun to lean and there was a growing crowd of sightseers enjoying the entertainment. Chris's perception was that the ketch was crewed by some rather haughty individuals and when Pirate George offered to give them a tow for £20 to clear the sand bar they declined, making it clear that a tow would be beneath them and they could manage on their own, 'Go away' one of them said.

The ketch's crew continued to try and free themselves to no avail and the tide meanwhile continued to ebb leaving them potentially even more stranded. Pirate George then offered to tow them off for £40. With poor grace they declined again. At this point he made the comment that for every 15 minutes of ebbing tide the price would go up by £20.

The ketch was finally towed off the bar for £100. That's five times the original offer and proved the age-old adage, when the pain gets great the price is right! Good old Pirate George!

This is not negotiable

When buyers use this tactic they might say, 'I have talked to my superiors; we have checked prices with your competitors, and this is all we are prepared to pay.' Or they might say, 'Don't give me your benefit story, we know what we are doing, this is our bottom line.' When a seller uses the same tactic, they might simply say, 'This is not negotiable.' Neither seller nor buyer should use these phrases because they usually produce anger and they show poor negotiating skills. When the buyer uses these phrases, the great temptation is to cave in to price.

One of my friends worked as salesman for a professional European consulting service. Their company policy meant that in most cases the seller would say, 'We do not negotiate' and would in fact walk away from the sale rather than do a deal. I understand their determination to hold on to price and not erode profits. However, one in two of those that walked away could have been saved with a gesture that would enable them to save face.

You could say in a situation like that, 'Company policy does not enable me to offer any kind of discount; however, *if you... then we...*' Maybe you could offer a small PC-based piece of software for them to develop your service, or a manual, or a reference book. There has to be a way for them to save face.

When our counterpart uses this phrase, we have two options: we either succumb to pressure on price, or handle it. If we are to handle it, we must give them a face-saving way out, otherwise we produce deadlock.

We can say, for example, 'I would like to take it but it's just not possible. However, *if you could do this... we could do that...*'

If a buyer says, 'Is your fee negotiable?', we say, 'We are happy to listen to any constructive suggestions you may have about the overall proposal.' My company was approached recently, and I was asked to be a keynote speaker at a business conference in Milton Keynes. I quoted my fee, and there was a telling silence. The other person began to negotiate, suggesting that I might like to do the seminar free, in return for a number of business opportunities. When I made it clear that it was not really of interest, he asked the next obvious question: 'Is your fee negotiable?' My answer was straightforward: 'I'm happy to look at this constructively – one of my colleagues would be interested in the business opportunities, he is prepared to come and speak and the cost will be significantly lower.' He got a lower price but he had to take a different proposal.

It is worth negotiating, worth hanging in there, and if we give them a face-saving way out, our opposite number will either back off or moderate their approach, if they see that we legitimately defend our price.

Don't ever assume that anything is not negotiable.

What ifs

What if we treble our requirement? *What if* we could give a two-year agreement? As soon as our opponents use phrases like this, they are able to discover any slack in our price or in our approach and they will negotiate from it.

I travel a great deal in the Third World and love to sharpen my skills in street market negotiation. The principles are just the same. You can try them in your local antique shop. Having browsed around and shown a general interest, point to two items and say, 'I'm interested in your best price, *what if* I take both?' The answer comes back: 'One thousand pounds.' Point to the one you don't want and say, 'How much just for that one?' He says, 'Six hundred.' You say, 'Fine, I'll have the other one for £400.' You have established some slack, and created room for negotiation.

My eldest son and I are negotiating to buy shotgun cartridges. We ask one dealer, 'How much if we buy them by the box?' and he replies, 'Fifteen pence each.' We say, '*what if* we buy 1,000?' He replies, 'Twelve pence each.' We then ask, 'How many do you have in stock?' He replies, 'Twenty thousand.' We say, '*What if* we buy half your stock?' He says, 'Ten pence each.'

As the buyers, we have now established significant slack in what he charges. One thing is for certain: whatever price we get, we won't be paying 15p each. Any time you use this tactic as a buyer, you will of course discover slack in the price and you should negotiate from it. If you are the seller experiencing this tactic, then as a general rule don't shoot from the hip. Buy time and get back the control by asking 'W' questions. Ask about their application; identify any problems or constraints or obstacles that they may be encountering. Check on their time constraints; ask what it is that they are most concerned with. Ask about safety, cost savings in fuel efficiency, whatever you can ask. Ask what difficulties they have experienced with previous supply. Most importantly, ask what their usage is. A good way to do that is to ask in the past tense, such as 'What was your monthly consumption last year?'

From time to time, our counterpart will ask for a price breakdown. If they do, we may have to give it to them, but we should never be pressurised into pricing on the spot. We should come back with a price after we have carefully thought through the implications. Price things they can do low. Things that only we can do, price high. Don't be bound by tramlines of method that you have used in the past. But also be willing to stick by your revealed pricing method if they want to adjust their total requirement.

I priced a marketing audit for a prospect. In my price I included a sum for both myself and one of my senior clinicians to do the brief together and to write the plan jointly. The same senior clinician was included in the price to provide helpline duties for 90 days. He also conducts telesales coaching immediately after the plan is presented.

The prospect understandably asked me to consider doing the audit alone, bringing in the senior clinician for the telesales work only. Because his rate is significantly lower than mine, I was able to demonstrate that taking him out of the briefing session would save a minuscule amount, for two reasons. First, he would now have to conduct a briefing session of his own for the telesales coaching. Second, the helpline content would dramatically increase in price because I would have to take that responsibility. The saving for the prospect was a few hundred pounds and the loss of input would far outweigh the minimal saving available. The prospect saw it immediately.

Deadlines

The other person can put a time deadline into the negotiation to try to pressure us into accepting lower terms than we would otherwise have done.

If you are on the receiving end, don't just accept stated deadlines – negotiate them. Many of us do it all the time, for example with hotel rooms. Just about every hotel, for example, requires that you vacate your bedroom by 12 noon. They put it into print, trying to enhance their authority. I rarely leave before 2 pm, often later than that, without paying any extra. You might say, 'I'm meeting some customers here for lunch – using your facilities – and I want to be able to change for a meeting shortly after that. I need to use my bedroom until then; I assume that is OK.'

As I write this chapter, I have just left the Toronto Sheraton, having conducted a seminar. I checked out at 3.45 instead of 12 noon simply by saying this: 'I ran two seminars here yesterday; would you please be gracious and extend my check-out time until 4 o'clock?' They wanted me to leave by 3 o'clock, so I settled finally by leaving at 3.45.

A buyer can use deadlines like these:

- **'Engineering insist that we agree this order by the weekend.'**
- **'My boss has to approve and I have a meeting scheduled with him for final signature in 30 minutes.'**
- **'It's now or never – we either agree right away or I will look elsewhere.'**
- **'Our client has insisted that we agree better terms from our suppliers this week.'**

What should the seller do in response? They should never accept the apparent urgency of the deadline and should always test it. 'I appreciate the importance of this to you but we will need four more days – I assume we can find a way round that?' If, having tested the deadline, it is real and immovable, you can still respond and save face by asking to call your office for confirmation.

There are some deadlines the seller can use either to pre-empt or counter this particular tactic:

- **'Our offer only lasts this week.'**
- **'Cost of materials increases this month, which means the price goes up on 1 February.'**
- **'If we don't agree to proceed by 1 February then we cannot produce the report by the end of February.'**
- **Or remember Pirate George and increase the price as the tide goes out. In other words make it clear that the price is dependent on time.**

7

Negotiable variables – or tradeable concessions

So far we have looked in different ways at the first four of our seven key elements: plan and prepare, rehearse, explore and explain, propose. Now we turn to the heart of all successful negotiation, the bargaining phase. Remember our definition: 'To bargain means to make it a condition of an agreement that something should be done.'

Bargaining means making any move on your part *conditional* on a move from your opposite number. There should never be any exception to this rule. It should be indelibly imprinted into our minds. Concessions must be traded with care. In simple terms, we never give assent to any concession until the other person has agreed what he or she will give in return.

Unskilled negotiators find a pressure to move quickly to give things away. If the other party has any sense, they will ask you for more, and the likelihood is that they will keep asking.

Never give, always trade

Never give something away without working out what it means to them. Never give something away without getting something back. And always ensure that what we give is seen as genuinely valuable or significant to our counterpart.

Never *give*, always *trade*. What I offer you must be balanced by what you offer me. Nothing is given away. *If we move* on any term, we must ensure that *the other person moves* towards us. Putting this into practice will automatically make you feel more authoritative. It will give you increasing confidence, and as you practise, it will quickly yield improving results.

Trade what is inexpensive to you

Ideally we aim to trade what is inexpensive to us and what is valuable to the other side. We must know the cost to us of any concession we make. We should know which things we can offer or trade that cost very little to us but which could be of high value to our opposite number.

Think this through carefully. Ask yourself, 'If I give this, what obstacle does it overcome, how much would that save?' Ask, 'What opportunity does this create for them or their company, what financial benefit could that bring them?' 'What preference does this satisfy?' 'What problem does this solve?' We ask ourselves what is this worth to them in savings, in productivity, in financial terms. The more specific we can be about the gain to the other party, the more valuable what we have to trade will appear to them.

One tradeable we can build in, which can cost us very little, is some form of guarantee. Guarantees often have high perceived value to the other person and yet may well cost us nothing. Let me illustrate. The public seminars we run at Insight Market have an unconditional money-back guarantee. If you are not totally satisfied with the value gained, we will refund your fees in full. In 15 years of training, fewer than 20 delegates have asked for their money back, so the guarantee has cost virtually nothing, but has high validity to a prospective delegate or host client company.

A variation of this technique was used by one of my associate companies, offering colour sales brochures. They would guarantee a minimum level of sales enquiries from these brochures, provided that they were used in a specific way with supporting documentation. They sold hundreds of brochures and telesales commissions. Not one company ever came back having failed to achieve the guaranteed result. But that was not the point; the point was that the guarantee had high perceived confidence and security value to the buyer. Was it low cost or low risk? Yes. In the unlikely event of any customer not achieving the promised levels of business, one of the company's many telesales staff would get on the phone for a few hours and generate the promised level of enquiries. As a side effect it was a marvellous way to back-sell the telesales operation.

Ask yourself what guarantees you could offer as part of your negotiation process – guarantees that are low cost and low risk to us, but high value to the other party. The technique applies equally when we are in buying mode. What can we guarantee as a buyer? For example; 'We are prepared to consider three years' repeat purchase subject to your company remaining competitive and your quality staying consistently at our Ship To Stock Standard. If we could agree to that, we would expect the following from you.' Remember, never give, always trade.

One of my associates was selling PC notebook computers to hotel chains on a 'roll-out' programme. At six to seven venues, these notebooks had to be delivered on the previous night, to the host hotel, configured in batches of eight to ten. The customer was negotiating hard on price. My associate used the guarantee as part of her concession trading: 'We can't adjust the price but what we can do is to have a technician at the hotel the previous night, taking responsibility for the security of the PCs. He will ensure that they are not only configured but in full running order so that from the first minute your salespeople can be trained. *There will be a guarantee* in this way of absolutely no error on the day – on condition that we get a signed agreement now.' The deal was agreed.

Don't give goodwill concessions

Some trainers use the term 'goodwill concession' to describe one-way movement on your part for which you have not asked for any return. Why do unskilled negotiators wrongly do this? Such concessions are often given incorrectly to get the negotiation concluded, or even to start it in the first place. The reality is that it makes your counterpart stronger.

These concessions are often given out of insecurity or discomfort, usually because of lack of knowledge about what to do. That's why it is so important to develop our negotiating skills. This is most typical with business owners who do not enjoy selling, marketing or negotiation. They have made a proposal, calculated the price, the other person seems reasonable and appears to have a need for the service, but the final agreement seems stuck. Out of simple naïveté or often out of frustration, the business owner will give a concession out of purported goodwill.

This is wrong, and seriously so. First, the other person will take advantage of the concession and invariably ask for more. Second, the profit level of the job is now eroded and will affect the owner, his or her staff, perhaps even the company's viability. Third, it will affect the owner's motivation for this job, for this client. It will leave a sour taste that need not have been there. The hard fact is that it was the owner's lack of competence and no fault of the other party. The more damaging long-term impact is the erosion of confidence in the owner's own business skills – all so easily rectified.

These one-way movements are sometimes given 'to get the deal moving'. Of course movement is essential, but it must always be two-way. A good phrase to handle this situation is '*If you... then we will...*' These four words are the nearest we will get to a magic phrase, because they force us to trade and not give. They always facilitate a response.

One-way movement like this creates a precedent that will rear its head every subsequent time you negotiate with the same person. They will expect it from you, and you will be weakened by the historic fact and the current pressure it is placing you under.

8

Rules for making concessions

Trade in small steps

Be stingy. When we offer something, make the other person work for it. Trade concessions reluctantly, one by one. It makes buyers think they have got to our bottom line. We need to avoid making larger concessions as the negotiation progresses; in fact each concession should be smaller than the one before. That means of course that we have listed our concessions beforehand. We know already which ones are first on our list and we work through them one at a time. Don't indicate that there are more, otherwise you will be pressed for more.

Trade concessions one at a time

We live in an age of time pressure. Often, negotiations are damaged because we rush in and give away too much, too soon. With busy managers, owners, partners, there is a tendency to give away a large concession, to speed up and conclude the negotiation process. You may even be thinking, 'This negotiation is not really worth this much time, there is so much else to do.'

A better way of viewing the same situation is to calculate how much time has already gone into this negotiation: your technical people, your presentation, your revisions and, not least, the amount of time you have already put in. All this is at risk because the pressure of time is urging you to come up with a solution now. There may even be an issue of personal confidence here. You may want a quick and apparently successful outcome to boost your own confidence. Resist it. Remember your predetermined commitment; bite your tongue and trade concessions one by one – slowly.

You might say, 'I need to reflect, I need to talk to...' What we think of our skill depends on how the bargaining goes. When we reach agreement too quickly, we later think we are a lousy negotiator.

Remember how we saw earlier, 'Never say yes first time.' This applies to the trading of concessions. When either buyer or seller reaches agreement too quickly, they will wonder whether they made a mistake or not. When you feel under any pressure to say 'Yes', say 'No' and buy some time.

Aim higher than you think

I give you this heading slightly tongue in cheek. But the truth is that most people worry about how low they should start, rather than how *high* they should aim. 'Aim higher and you will come out better' – all the trainers say that. 'How much higher?' is the age-old question. 'Test it' is the answer. You will never know whether you could get more until you have asked for more.

People often ask me, 'How much should I charge for my time, my product, my service?' There are some simple tests you can run, to check the impact of price. You compare with other similar offerings in your market, you ask yourself about your own confidence in your pricing levels. Ask yourself if there is some way in which you can package your product or service to put it into a different league.

You can test with direct mail. Send out an offer with tests on, say, four different prices. Monitor the response and see what percentage return you get with each test price. You may find that all four yield the same return. That would indicate that there is still more room for price movement. You may find that price 4 – the highest – yields just half the response of price 2, which is exactly half the price. Then you have a value judgement: do I want fewer customers at the higher price – maybe less invoicing, less administration. Or do I want more customers at a lower price because I have other things I can sell them?

Make sure you have a clear rationale for the price you ask, and communicate it with strength and conviction. Here again the USP (or the more developed MDSA©) will work for you. The stronger it is, the more measurable its effect, the better your chances for higher pricing. At least by aiming high you give yourself maximum room to negotiate.

Sales people can test with their face to face appointments. A good average conversion ratio of appointments to new business is 4:1. If your ratio is 2:1 or 3:1 it is almost certainly because your price is too low. It is crying out, 'Test me with a higher price'. If your conversion ratio is 4:1 you might like to test higher prices until your conversion worsens and then make a value judgement – less orders at a higher price, or more orders at a lower price.

If a buyer presses you on price, it may be because they are not convinced that your service is worth what you are asking. That means that your USP is not clear, not relevant or miscommunicated. Alternatively, if they think your services are very valuable, they may be willing to pay a great deal more for it than they tell you they are.

If you are in buying mode, it often works well to ask for a shocking discount, well over what any reasonable person would expect. Give yourself room. Whether we are buying or selling, remember it is very difficult to trade up. If we aim higher than we think, it is very easy to trade down.

Don't split the difference

Of all the tactics in negotiation, this one is probably the most commonly used. Even the most inexperienced person will resort to this tactic. Why? Because it resolves a potential sticking point and brings agreement nearer in what appears to be a 'fair' manner. It is an apparently easy way out for the inexperienced negotiator and provides a face-saving way out for both parties.

Don't split the difference. Let's say we are buying. We want to buy at £80k and our seller wants £90k. They may well say, 'Let's split the difference.' Don't settle for £85k. If the other person uses the phrase 'Let's split the difference', our answer will be, 'We couldn't afford to do that, but I'll tell you what we could do. If you will... then we will...'

This tactic is commonly applied by both buyer and seller. It is attractive because it brings the end in sight. We can often succumb because of the apparently reachable agreement. If we respond and simply split the difference, then we will lose money. We should trade a concession and without doubt improve our deal. Price is usually the last thing we want to trade, so we must have other things ready to trade first.

As a buyer, even if you ultimately have to shift on price, you will end up moving to £82k and not £85k. That one skill alone has just saved your company £3,000.

One of my clients was negotiating a large sale where the customer was obliged to pay up front for a 12-month supply. The customer was very concerned about paying up front for 12 months and was more than a little nervous about the credibility of the company. He asked for two months' trial supply. This is never acceptable, simply because the service takes six months' usage before results show positively. My client thought to himself, 'I will meet him halfway' and offered a six-month trial on condition that signed agreement was reached that day. Both of them accepted, and to be honest, both were wrong. They had effectively split the difference. What he should have done was to ask for more; he had given too much too soon. The buyer responded wrongly in accepting the split difference; he should have responded, 'I can't do that, but what I can do is...'

Watch out for the shocker

I shall never forget the moment. My wife and I were buying a house. It was advertised on the market for £230,000 and my wife suggested, 'Why don't you shock them with an offer of £140,000? In fact,' she said, 'if I phone them and offer £135,000, will you give me the saved £5,000 for the garden?' I assented and she made the call. They were duly shocked. But we settled to my amazement at £135,000!

Why did we do that? There was nothing to lose. If we had been unsuccessful, we could still have come back with a sensible offer nearer their original asking figure. Using a shocking opening position can quickly find any slack. When someone tries it on you, be prepared. If you are ready for it, you won't get angry and walk out!

Say, 'Thank you for your offer. As you can imagine, this is not even close. I will leave this for now and ask if you would kindly reflect on it. Maybe I can come back to you to see if it would be possible to find a way forward.'

We have kept the relationship intact. We have given them a face-saving way back into the negotiation, but we have defended our price. Often in response they will laugh and say, 'Just checking, now what would be close?' That is a very good ploy if you are buying, because it now gently coerces the seller to state a view on price that hopefully has been leveraged downwards.

If you are selling, you might say, 'I would like to come back to that in just a moment, but what I would like to do first is to run through an outline of the whole proposed deal.'

The shocker can work particularly well when you have done your plan and prepare, and in your research discovered factors which open up the door of possibility for this tactic.

Having done their homework, two friends of mine made a

shocking offer on the price of a flat. The flat had been on the market for £180,000 but they had researched and discovered the seller was a housing development company a few weeks away from year end with a cash shortage. They also discovered that three previous sales had fallen through probably because of mortgage problems. They offered to complete within a guaranteed three week window but offered only £100,000 in cash. After some hesitation the development company accepted the offer. The plan and prepare stage gave my friends the confidence to use the shocker, and to use it effectively.

Don't be first to accede to pressure on primary items

Never be the first to concede on *primary* items. Always begin on *secondary* items. We know from our analysis which concessions are primary and which secondary. Try to ensure that your counterpart is the first to yield on a primary point. Remember that this negotiation will end at some position between your ideal and theirs. The closer to your ideal you can get, the better off you are. If you make the first primary concession, the chances are that the negotiation will swing more in your opponent's favour, simply because we have given something too large or too valuable too soon.

We are endeavouring all the time to 'match and trade'. That is why it is so important to trade carefully. If you feel that you are getting close to exhausting your secondary options, ask for something primary in return for a secondary move of your own. But never match a primary concession of your own for a secondary one of theirs.

This gets particularly acute as a deadline nears. Be particularly watchful when deadlines of any sort are involved. You may well find yourself ensnared by a deadline that you imposed earlier in the negotiation process. You can buy yourself time by suggesting that you call your office to see whether there is any way that the deadline could be extended by minutes, hours or even days.

Help the other person to feel they have a good deal

When we finish the negotiation and come to agreement, it is very important to the fulfilment of the agreement reached, and the long-term relationship involved, that we don't gloat over any apparent victory. Remembering our maxim of win–win, we should be at pains to help the other party feel that they have a good deal. Good negotiators will also ensure that wherever possible the counterpart in reality has got a good deal from their perspective.

If you were buying, and your seller feels one or more of the following, they will feel positive about the outcome, and will feel they have a bargain:

- **if they feel they have done better than their competitors;**
- **if the price is good for them in terms of profit, volume delivery, etc;**
- **if they are confident in your prompt payment and supplier loyalty;**
- **if they have extracted some form of 'guarantee' from you;**
- **if they feel there is a genuinely good chance of future business.**

Whether you are the buyer or seller, tell the other party that they are real professionals. Build their respect and affirmation. It will also build their appreciation and respect for you.

If you were selling, why not write or e-mail your buyer, congratulating them on the terms they have secured. Affirm in writing some of the key points that they have negotiated and affirm your commitment to service and customer care. Talk about your pleasure at welcoming them as a customer and build in positive comments about the anticipated long-term relationship. Why not even send some personalised and appropriate greeting card. Helping the counterpart feel good can be as simple as giving them unexpectedly 'one more than they expected'. 'One more' can be one more anything.

I was speaking at a public seminar in the United States. A building contractor in Miami was telling me how after he finishes every job – when the snagging terms have been negotiated and agreed – he always gives one more thing. What he usually does is to landscape some small area or plant some special trees – free – as his way of saying thank you. He has been doing that for 18 years and has kept many of his clients for the whole of that time. They obviously felt they got a good deal.

Maximise the value of what you offer

Emphasise the value of what you are offering. We do this by emphasising the apparent cost to us, using phrases like 'That would create a precedent' or 'That would be very difficult'.

If there is no apparent or believable cost to us, we are really conceding or trading nothing in the mind of our opponent.

The more we can maximise the true value of what we have to offer, the greater the concession appears to be. Here is a simple checklist to help establish the value of any concession we make:

- **Make it clear, where appropriate, that it is very difficult to give – for example, because of your superior technology, the technicalities of the process involved or the cost involved.**
- **Where it helps your case, quantify that cost, and multiply it up – for example, the cost per annum, the cost if every buyer or user had the same arrangement.**

By doing this you can quite easily make it appear totally unreasonable and in doing so lower their aspiration.

- **Refer to major problems solved, or obstacles removed.**
- **Refer to savings gained and quantify wherever possible.**
- **Refer to past gains either for this company or for other companies, which you can use as testimonial material.**
- **Clarify that this is not your company policy.**
- **Refer to opportunities that it can open up.**
- **Refer to preferences it can satisfy.**
- **In all of this, remember to use MDSA©.**

Minimise the value of what they are offering

Lower in their mind the value of what they are offering. Reduce the cost to them. 'Surely you would incur that cost anyway?' Reduce their perception of the apparent value to us: 'That's of no real value to us', or 'That's of little value to us'. Reduce their aspirations; their concessions need to appear meaningless.

Where we can genuinely use this, here is a simple checklist to help reduce the impact of what they believe they are offering us by way of concession:

- **Treat it as if it is not a real concession. Make them feel that it is like vapourware.**
- **Suggest that it is only what is expected in cases like these.**
- **Suggest that they would incur those costs anyway – implying no extra cost.**
- **Suggest that other companies you deal with, give and often give more.**
- **Suggest that you have the potential benefits of this concession already.**

Don't just think it!

At the end of this bargaining or trading phase, always summarise the details. Restate all the points of agreement and summarise what they contain. Write them down and let the other party see what you have written. Turn the paper round so that it is facing them. But make sure that you voice it all – *speak it out*. This applies to maximising or minimising the effect of concessions. Don't just think about how valuable your concession is. Don't just think about how insignificant their response is. *Say it, and say it clearly.*

Looking for negotiable variables

We must stop seeing price as the key issue. The most common mistake made by inexperienced negotiators is a default preoccupation with price. We must learn a change of mindset where we don't think price and where we do think negotiable variable. In other words, our minds need to be full of all the variables surrounding each potential deal. Best of all are the ones cheap to us and valuable to the counterpart.

Find areas for negotiable variables

We have seen their importance but now we have to come up with some. How do we go about determining where our negotiable variables lie? How do we determine them and evaluate their relative worth? The following checklist is a helpful starting point:

- **The product or service itself – ask yourself: How could it be changed? What elements can be added or removed? What are the implications to the other party in terms of cost, longevity, quality, etc?**

- **What specific functions or attributes does it have – do they vary with different applications or in different markets?**
- **The impact of promotion or publicity that surrounds it.**
- **Expenditure. Think through implications of the manner of payment: credit terms or direct debits; discounts; progress payments and pre-payments.**
- **Volume. Think through implications of packaging, storage, insurance. Who pays for what?**
- **Quality. What does quality mean and to whom? Can you substantiate cost additions or reductions for varying levels of quality? Can you quantify what variations mean to your counterpart – what they might be worth to them?**
- **Delivery arrangements (amounts, locations, frequency).**
- **Maintenance, service or after-sales care.**
- **Guarantees or warranties.**

Identify key variables and their place in the negotiation

Having located the general area of where we can find these concessions or tradeable variables, we must now home in and identify more accurately how we can use them.

Seven key questions emerge here:

1. What concessions do we normally make?
2. What is their value to our counterpart? Have we quantified that value in measurable terms?
3. What would we like to have in return?
4. What other tradeables do we have?
5. What could we concede that costs us little but has high value to our counterpart?
6. What can they reciprocate that may be low cost to them but valuable to us?

7. What negotiable variables could we build into our offer/ proposal in the first place?

From these prompts, make sure that you have taken the time to list all your tradeables, your negotiable variables. You should have a typed list of up to 20 of them. You should know how much they cost per month, or per year. You should know the impact on your cost or profit of each of these concessions – even multiplied by the number of customers that you have. You should have a clear idea of their value to your counterpart.

Build in some negotiable variables

When you have exhausted your list of current actual tradeables, ask yourself what other negotiable variables you could build in that you don't yet have. The answer lies in discovering what you could add to your product, service or offering, perhaps bundling it into a package and then peeling off certain non-essential layers as tradeable concessions.

Alternatively, you evaluate the tradeables and, if they are fairly low cost to you, add them as concessions that you can trade, in return for something else from your counterpart.

My main business is in training and consultancy and I regularly conduct strategic marketing reviews for small to medium-size companies. What I have done is to build in some negotiable variables. One of them is a helpline that gives qualified telephone back-up support to the implementation process of the plan produced.

Another variable is a health check at six-monthly intervals. I can build them into the original offer and then use them to trade. Or I can leave them out of the original offer and add them at the trading phase.

When I am buying, I am busy thinking about what negotiable variables I can conjure up for my potential suppliers. A good example of this comes from running seminars.

Most hotels have a so-called fixed rate – for full day only – for seminar rooms. I always ask them, 'What is your price for a full day?' They might say, '£800.' I say, 'I want it for a half-day only, I will be cleared out by 12 noon, I would like to book it for £350.' They usually splutter and mutter but I very rarely have to pay the full day rate even though that is printed policy.

I then turn to the tea and biscuits. I ask, 'How much for tea and biscuits?' They say, '£1.90 per person.' I say, 'I am running upwards of 100 seminars per year and many of your competitors will do just tea for £1 – can you better that, please?' A bit of trading then ensues, but I will not pay for the biscuits. That trading alone will save me or my sponsoring clients £5,000 or more per annum. Do that for 10 years and it has saved £50,000. I point out that fact to any reluctant conference manager and they are usually a little shocked and will usually make an appropriate reduction.

Determine whether this is long term or short term

A hunter goes out to get enough for the one meal; farming looks for a long-term ongoing supply. The rules are very different. If this negotiation is definitely a one-off deal, you can afford to be a hunter – more demanding, more insistent and more intent on your interests. Stalk your prey, make your kill and devour the proceeds.

In the main, however, we have to deal with the same people, the same companies over and over. It is much closer to farming. Farming is long term, looking for a return each year or each season. That means the deals we secure have to sustain a relationship over an extended period. In the process, we have to uncover negotiable variables that make sense for the other person in the long term as well as the short. Remember, we have to live out the consequences of our negotiation.

In our public events we will often ask the following question, 'How many times can you skin a sheep?' The response varies and is usually accompanied by a few bemused smiles. The answer of course is 'only once'. You can shear a sheep many times, arguably to the advantage of both parties, but you can only skin it once and then the poor thing is dead. It's a limited metaphor but shearing is closer to win–win and skinning very definitely win–lose!

Potential sources of negotiable variables

Looking more specifically at some of these sources of tradeables will help us to focus our aim and be more precise. These tradeables are not just good in the sense that they help us to achieve the agreement both parties are seeking, but in the process they are doubly helpful, in that they also produce long-term deals that stick. If both parties are motivated by the agreement then we are doubly successful.

Payment

There is so much scope for negotiation on terms – particularly in the United Kingdom, where there is considerable government lobbying on this very issue. Even our old friend the tax office is open to some honest negotiation when it comes to repaying overdue tax.

In 15 years of running this particular business I have never had one bad debt. How is that? Very simply, I always ask for a cheque on the day, with every new client, and a cheque on the last day of the month for every long-term client. Very few have ever queried paying on the day. It has the advantage of being related close in time to the services rendered. In other words, in my field – seminars – people are usually highly motivated at the end of the seminar and it is not painful for them to part with the money. One month or two months later a lot of that feel-good factor will have been dissipated by the normal daily grind.

Why not say, '*If you* can give us a cheque on the day rather than your 60-day terms, we can provide a further half-day of helpline time.' Consultants, and professionals like accountants, why not negotiate your payment on direct debit: say, '*If we can agree* monthly direct debits starting this month *then we can reduce* the annual fee by £800.'

Buyers use payment terms creatively. Very few sellers do. You can actually motivate others to trade concessions by the simplest of adjustments to payment.

Caution: Do not ever accept normal practice as binding. As long as it is ethical, there is no reason whatever for you to be bound by years of so-called normal – in reality, damaging – practice.

Quantity

Think through the implications of volume on your buying or selling. If it is a product, perhaps you say, '*I can* lower the price from X *if you take* Y.' If you are a consultant, say, '*We can* provide the research for £1,000 per annum each office, rather than £1,200 *if you* include your regional offices.'

If you are the buyer, think creatively about how you can use volume to your advantage. You might say, 'How important is volume to you; at what point does increased volume impact your production – positively or negatively?' This can apply to the purchase of fixed-price items that have become virtual commodities.

I was buying a new PC for my office. I knew from previous experience that asking for a discount did not work, but I talked about volume and discovered that if you bought 12 you could get one free. It then became an option for me to act as a coordinator for some of my friends and acquaintances in buying bulk.

Time

There are all kinds of factors that can be considered. Think of the timing of delivery, further shipments, progress reports, closing dates, deadlines. Think through the time-related elements of your own sale or purchase and use those elements to advantage.

A number of my clients run subscription-based services, where the contract is an annual membership fee. It is quite costly to renew these customers each year and there are some genuine savings if a customer will agree to a two- or three-year contract. It makes sense to offer something for those extended agreements when necessary.

Another variation is offered by the Marketing Guild, which has a nominal annual membership fee payable by direct debit on a 'till forbid' basis. If you will sign up on a standing order at one of the public events, they will refund the entire cost of that day's event.

A useful way to probe for a concession is to say, '*We will accept your figure if you make it* a three-year contract instead.' Or, '*We will agree your figure if you agree* to a six-monthly implementation review.'

When you are in buying mode, think through some variables that you could beneficially use. If you know you need the product or service for three or more years, why not suggest, 'We could pay you what you are asking but not quite yet. What we could do is pay 90 per cent of your asking price this year, 95 per cent next year and your current quoted price in year three. If that was acceptable, we could sign a three-year contract subject to conditions.'

More or less?

An obvious way to trade is to add or remove items from the agreement. It may work for you to have more, it may work for them to have less.

The art is to think these through before the negotiation starts so that you are crystal clear about the cost or profit implications. For example, '*If you will* agree to a quarterly review, *we can* reduce the audit fee by 10 per cent. *If you let us* supply all your TVs both for sale and rental, *we will add digital* to each unit.'

Creative buying instincts can quickly find a use for these tradeables. '*If you can agree* this price adjustment on our corporate brochure, *we will commit ourselves* to take 500 A4 flyers at your list price.' This works even better if you know from the beginning that the 500 flyers have to be bought from somewhere. Doing your homework here will pay dividends.

There are all kinds of options open to us if we will think creatively about the specification of our requirement or our product/service. One way to test is to say, '*If we can eliminate* this area, then *we can accept* your proposal of £10,000. *If we can reduce* the desk research, *then we can adjust* the price.'

You say, 'You can have the manuals, if we can have two months to write your plan rather than three weeks.' If they say, 'No, we certainly can't do that', you have discovered that time is a key issue. That information then tells you what is highly valuable to them and often what is low cost to you. You can then trade more intelligently.

A strategy for referrals

In our training we encourage clients to adopt a simple strategy for referrals by asking their customers for referrals routinely, every three months. A marvellous technique is to build it in as a negotiable. This should be high on our list of favourites because it costs nothing and yet has a very high real and perceived value. If you are selling, why not use it like this: '*I'll agree* to the price you want, *if you arrange* a presentation with...' Could be another branch, another division or a colleague in another company with a similar usage or requirement. Or 'We will agree to this very special pricing structure, if you will invite 10 other potential users to your factory, and act as a positive reference site. We will also feel free to bring prospective clients of our own to the site at mutually agreed frequencies and at arranged times.'

One of my friends developed a marvellous sales tracking software, with macros for sales letters, recalls and networked fax applications. His company negotiated to develop it for a local company at cost. They did this simply because they wanted a multi-user reference site that had networked fax application. They ultimately invited a number of prospects to the site, including an international distributor. The distributor was so impressed that they incorporated the software into their suite of programs and their national distribution programme.

An international software company asked me to run an in-house programme. They specifically wanted me rather than someone else from our team of presenters. I used this approach: 'I will present this first programme along with one of my senior associates if you will be willing to refer her to other departments and teams within the organisation, providing of course you are totally happy with the outcome of the day.'

One great negotiating idea for referrals comes into play when clients cannot pay their bills on time. This is a significant area for negotiation skills and the first priority for your own cash flow must be to endeavour to get payment moving positively towards you. But even then, remember the maxim to think of all the variables, not just the £s.

As I write this third edition, in a recession, we have had some long-term faithful clients who are struggling to pay. These clients are friends who have been using our services and up to the recession have been good payers. Now they are struggling; they want to pay and simply cannot. One of the variables has been to get them to become active ambassadorial referral centres. We have had them travel and stand up in our public events endorsing our service from their own experience. The results have been extremely potent. We are still working on their payments too!

The magic 'if'

Did you notice all the emphasised words in italics in the preceding pages? Let me highlight them for you:

- **'I can... *if* you take...'**
- **'We can... *if* you...'**
- **'We will accept... *if* you will make...'**
- **'We will agree... *if* you agree...'**
- **'*If* you can... we can...'**
- **'*If* you let us... we can...'**
- **'*If* we can agreee... then we can reduce...'**
- **'I'll agree... *if* you will arrange...'**
- **'*If* we can eliminate... we can accept...'**
- **'*If* we can reduce... then we can adjust...'**

You spotted the 'magic' word – *if*. It is in every sentence that forms part of our trading phase. We always use '*if*' every time we make a proposal. It makes it clear that movement is expected and puts gentle pressure on that movement.

If tells your counterpart the price of your revised offer, or the price of your movement. If they want something from you, it will cost them, and the 'magic *if*' makes that very clear.

Use silence

It is quite all right to have silence; you are not obliged to talk. The fact is, the one who talks more gives more away. The more you talk, the more information you are likely to be giving the other person. That information increases his or her authority in the negotiation – every time!

If you get thrown at any time – and it happens to the most experienced – give yourself time to think. Ask to use the phone, take a loo break. Tell them you need a bit of fresh air and ask for 15 minutes. Or just sit in silence doodling or writing on your paper. If they get embarrassed, don't let it worry you; tell them what is going on and say, 'Excuse me while I think this through for a few moments', or ' Excuse me, I just need a few moments of silence while I calculate the impact of this for both of us.'

If you are negotiating on the telephone, silence is a useful ploy. The other party feels compelled to break it.

Equally, when the deal is agreed, don't hang around. Many a good deal has been badly damaged by the talking that ensued. Many of you will find a propensity to verbal diarrhoea at this point. The reason is that there has been so much control, so much pent-up energy. But if you lose the deal here, you can lose it in a big way.

I remember negotiating one deal for a client. I had an experienced technical person with me. He knew his role and he was brilliant, he let me lead. He only contributed when I drew him in. But I forgot to tell him what to do at the end. As soon as the deal was struck he thought the rules had changed. He began discussing at length how he would overcome certain technical problems. Those problems had not even surfaced during the negotiation. Weeks of work, and thousands of pounds were blown with just a few minutes' careless words.

10

Handling deadlock

Deadlock is one of the most counterproductive and undesirable of all the conclusions to a negotiation. We should be alert for its possibilities and try to avoid it. The only exception is where we threaten deadlock as a tactic to galvanise our counterpart into action.

The main cause of deadlock is the absence of sufficient negotiable variables being used. The more variables you can arm yourself with at the start, the less likely it is that you will be deadlocked.

Watch out for frustration

Reaching a deadlock is a frustrating experience. Usually, a lot of time has gone into the negotiation. You may have already made one or two visits, your proposals have been put together with hours of work and now you have deadlock. One of the biggest dangers is that you will react badly out of frustration, particularly if this is a large deal and you are getting tired. We can see this illustrated often, when trade unions and employers have long, arduous negotiating sessions, day and night. When there is deadlock it produces a certain type of aggression that causes one or both parties to make unwise statements or unwise moves.

Be aware of it, be prepared for it and be careful how you act when in the middle of it.

Avoid immovable positions

We can get to the situation where neither party feels able to budge. At this point a new dynamic occurs, in the sense that you and your opposite number are now opponents rather than counterparts. If you dig in and declare a firm unalterable position, it is more than likely that they will too. Immovable positions should be avoided to prevent deadlock.

A builder had quoted a fixed price for a loft conversion. One particular aspect was the staircase. The local building regulation department proved unusually fussy and insisted on some specific changes to the staircase as the drawing specification was unacceptable. Extra charges were incurred, not just on the revised staircase itself, but on all the fittings required. Deadlock was imminent. In a case like this, if you are belligerent, the customer will invariably put his or her foot down and insist that the builder absorb all the costs. The builder would equally expect the customer to pay all. Immovable positions are taken and deadlock looms.

A better way is to review the whole project positively with the client. It's his home, his project. Ask the client his opinion, what he likes and dislikes. Ask him if he would be willing to pay a little extra for something that would end up significantly better. Is he willing to enhance the whole ship for a ha'penny worth of tar? Exploring a whole variety of options can save the day when the client would otherwise have dug in his heels.

The builder in this case should have the ideal in mind and a minimum acceptable figure as his bottom line.

Avoid price rot

Sometimes, however, and more commonly in business negotiations, buyers threaten deadlock to panic sellers into price rot. This is a dreadful disease – painful and sometimes terminal. Buyers threaten sellers with a phrase like 'Unless we can agree to this price reduction, I see no way forward.'

Sellers can succumb to the threat, and in doing so rot their price structure for ever. They can dig their own heels in, declare an immovable position, and counter-threat. That is not always wrong; it can call their counterpart's bluff. Most appropriately, they can defend their price but trade concessions.

The moral is simple: don't allow the threat of deadlock to panic you into price rot as a seller, or a price hike if you are the buyer. How do we avoid that in practice? Well, we need a bridge.

The bridging moment

We can do ourselves and the long-term relationship a great deal of good if we can calmly take control, but in a manner that clearly has both parties' best interests at heart.

We achieve that by moving into the bridging moment, and we handle the deadlock with a phrase like this: 'Mr or Ms Counterpart, we have both put a lot of effort into this; let us have one more go before we admit defeat.' Or, 'There is real value in the time and effort that have gone in from both sides, so could we look at this one more time?' And then begin asking W questions again, open-ended questions.

Alternatively, we can use the bridging moment to agree positively on what we have determined, to buy a little bit of time, then summarise where we feel the negotiation has moved forward positively. Write down the key points in summary form. Then use a bridging phrase like this: 'It seems we are both pleased with the points of agreement we have covered, but clearly we have an area here where there seems to be no possibility of progress today. Can I suggest that we agree another meeting, say in one week, when we have both had time to reflect creatively? How does that sound?'

Or you might suggest, 'It may help both of us if we break here and work *informally* on heads of agreement, and come back together *informally* next week. How does that sound?' Emphasising the informal context is often enough to get the process moving again. It takes the intensity out of the moment, gives time for reflection, and enables both parties to save face. It takes the high pressure of formal commitment out of the equation for now. Both parties are likely to be more relaxed, and that one thing alone may well save the moment.

Make a statement – ask a question

Whether you are making one more attempt now to break the deadlock, or are meeting informally later, this key skill will enable you to move the process forward. It is an accepted fact that whoever is asking questions is in control. Being in control is your responsibility. If you want to be effective in your negotiation, the only way you can maintain that control at this point is by making an acceptable statement and then following it with a series of W questions.

W questions are absolutely vital, simply because they are your only chance of getting the buyer talking again. For example: 'We are going to come back again informally; could I ask, what do you feel most strongly about? What in your opinion could change our problem? How would you feel about a 24-month option? What is it that you do like about our proposal?' You may well find in some cases that this technique enables you fairly easily and naturally to go back to negotiating again.

Whether it does or doesn't, the W questions will give you information that can enhance the process of reflection which will now have to take place.

The way forward

One of the reasons for extra tension is that when deadlock occurs, we are unprepared for it and simply don't know what the correct procedure is. To simplify it for ourselves, there are only three productive outcomes possible. Either we have one more attempt at negotiation there and then, or we meet later at an agreed time to discuss our reflected views *informally*. Or we meet again in a more *formal* setting.

Whichever of the three is chosen, it is vital that you keep positive, and communicate in a positive manner. Before you part, make sure you have documented a brief summary of agreement so far. You may well be able to document the particular issues that you will need to reflect on or report informally on. Where you have asked W questions, you may want to jot down the key concerns that you have un- covered. If your counterpart has uncovered concerns of yours, jot them down as well. Reaffirm your commitment to work for a solution. Reaffirm your desire to do business with your counterpart. Thank them for their effort and energy. The next chapter details specific techniques for asking questions.

When you get back to the office, word process your summary notes and fax or e-mail them to your counterpart. Make sure that you repeat your commitment to arriving at a mutually beneficial agreement.

One alternative, as a last resort, would be to jointly agree two other negotiators to have an informal chat. It could be your MDs or your technical directors. The latter is risky, and you would have to ensure that they were reasonably competent and also that they were thoroughly briefed.

11

Questions, questions, questions

Questioning – an overview

Many aspiring negotiators make the mistake of doing all the talking. We need to ASK, ASK, ASK, until it becomes second nature to ask questions, and listen for the answer. It is written somewhere, 'Be quick to listen and slow to speak.' One of my earliest mentors used to say to me, 'Oliver, you have two ears and one mouth; you need to learn to use them in that proportion.'

Let's face it, the less you say, the more relevant you are likely to be. Let me ask you a few questions myself. If you are talking, who are you normally talking about? Of course the answer is 'yourself'. That produces a defensive or bored response in the counterpart. Worse still, you will inevitably be giving away information that they can use to their advantage.

Questions make the difference

What would you think is at the heart of so-called consultative activity – what makes it consultative? The answer? Questions –

but not just any questions, questions that help the prospect discover for themselves their needs and wants. Questions stop us presenting our full story too soon.

My kids complained recently about the size of my glasses. They were concerned that they looked like 'patio doors'. So off I trotted to the opticians. The clinician – the consultant – put me through the usual rigmarole: hard chair, strange lights, uncomfortable seating position. We went through red and green circles, oxo and crosshairs. She sat me in front of an intimidating-looking piece of machinery and without warning squirted some strange liquid in my eyes. At the end of this reasonably intolerable performance she said, and I quote, 'Mr Oliver, you need vari-focals.' It made me angry, and as I left the consulting room I made up my mind to stay with the patio doors and just put in some new windows.

I went through to the fitter with my mind made up, but watch what happened. He began to ask me about my work, how big were the seminars, did I use my notes frequently and did I interact with my delegates? Then he asked me this one question: 'Mr Oliver, when you have been interacting with your delegates and then you come back to your podium, do you find it takes you quite a long time these days to focus on your notes?' What has he done? He has acted as the real consultant by asking incisive, penetrative questions that have my good at heart. Questions give us a consultative air that will add to our authority and add to what we uncover from the counterpart. And just in case you're feeling smug and saying to yourself, 'I am never as bad as the clinician in the story', let's remember that all she did wrong was to present the solution before she had uncovered the real value.

Asking questions is the method of navigation

The primary key to staying in control is to ask questions.

Whoever is asking questions is by inference leading, directing, shaping. If at any moment in any phase, you feel that control is slipping from your grasp, make a statement, ask a question, and you are easily back in control. Asking questions is the only way you can find out what, other than price, is really important to this individual or company. In a free market economy there are only two pivotal points around which a deal is ultimately agreed: 1) price; 2) the benefit, advantage or gain that your counterpart could experience as a result of agreeing the terms.

Asking appropriate questions is the only way you can uncover what your counterpart feels, needs or wants in the area of benefit, advantage or gain. To put it another way, the questions you ask and the resultant answers demonstrate the criteria by which your counterpart will evaluate your proposal or bargaining process.

Asking intelligent questions implies that you will have competent solutions or answers. Asking questions is the only way that you can express interest in your counterpart's goals, needs, objectives and aspirations. Asking questions will give you information that others do not have, information that will build your authority and give you the edge.

The outcome of questions

The person who asks questions is:

1. leader at that point (whoever asks the questions is in control);
2. determining the REAL REASONS for buying;
3. automatically treated as knowledgeable – consultative professional (think of examples like doctors and lawyers);
4. perceived to be genuinely interested in me and my problem – not just his or her own ends.

- **Only questions will give you the information you need, to match with the right benefits.**

- **Asking questions will give you information that others don't have – information that will give you an edge.**
- **The professional asks questions. The amateur gives answers.**
- **The questions that we ask give us the ability to be motivators rather than manipulators.**
- **Ask the prospect if you could ask a number of straightforward questions.**
- **Use silence and pauses.**
- **Ensure that you have a list of basic questions which you are developing as you go along.**

What sort of questions?

If questioning is so vital, what kind of questions should we be asking? We should be asking open-ended questions. Closed questions are questions to which the only answer is 'Yes' or 'No'. They produce no additional information, they close down the conversation, they close down the proper negotiation process too early. Typical closed questions are prefaced with 'Do you...?', 'Could you...?', 'Will you...?'

Open-ended questions cannot be answered 'Yes' or 'No'; they always produce a response and always yield information. In training circles they are loosely referred to as W questions. They include What?, Which?, When?, Where?, Why?, Who?, and the odd one out: How? They always generate information and they are key to retaining control at every stage of the negotiation process.

A builder had negotiated a deal with a Baptist church for renovation work valued at £120,000. The deal appeared to be agreed, but the architect simply would not give the builder the start date. The builder was stalled for some weeks and could not get a clear picture from the architect. In a move to get things under way, the MD of the building company approached the church direct and began asking W questions to attempt to discover the nature of the problem. It transpired that the church wanted to carry on meeting in the building while the renovations were going on. They had been told that it would not be possible. The builder simply offered to find alternative accommodation while the work was in hand – offering to pay for it himself. The cost of that was a few hundred pounds but would have the effect of releasing £120,000 of work.

Subsequently, with the goodwill his gesture generated, he was able to work out a method of working that enabled the church to carry on meeting – with some temporary facilities – within their existing premises. The job got under way.

An exercise

So far we have assumed that the prospect has a *felt requirement*. But suppose they don't. Suppose they are quite happy with their present arrangements. How many times have you been on a call and then felt stumped? You just did not know which way to go.

A possible way forward is to do one of two things: either a) uncover a problem and enlarge it to the point where they are willing to do something about it, or b) help them to see an opportunity that we can help them to achieve.

To help us focus our approach we use a consultative technique called FPOOP©. This will expose certain areas of weakness in our understanding or knowledge.

FPOOP© stands for

Fear

Preference

Obstacle

Opportunity

Problem

List any fears your prospect might have:

1.

2.

3.

4.

5.

6.

Now simply convert them into 'W' questions:

1.

2.

3.

4.

5.

6.

List any preferences your prospect might have:

1.

2.

3.

4.

5.

6.

Now convert them into 'W' questions:

1.

2.

3.

4.

5.

6.

List any potential opportunities your prospect might have:

1.

2.

3.

4.

5.

6.

Now simply convert them into 'W' questions:

1.

2.

3.

4.

5.

6.

List the potential obstacles your prospect might have:

1.

2.

3.

4.

5.

6.

Now convert them into 'W' questions:

1.

2.

3.

4.

5.

6.

List the potential problems your prospect might have:

1.

2.

3.

4.

5.

6.

Now convert them into 'W' questions:

1.

2.

3.

4.

5.

6.

What reasons could we use to convince the prospect that the problem you have uncovered is really serious?

1.

2.

3.

Can we convert these 'reasons' into questions?

Note: Arrange these questions in order of importance, ie which ones yield the most important information for your negotiating process. This means that if your counterpart does not allow you to ask all the questions, the key ones have been covered.

Remember, these are not intended to be 'perfect' or exhaustive. They are a start. You will change, add and delete in the light of experience and what works best for you.

Six summary reasons for asking questions

1. Helps you to avoid arguments.
2. Helps you to avoid talking too much.
3. Enables you to help the other party recognise what they want, then you can help them decide how to get it.
4. Helps crystallise the other party's thinking. The idea then becomes their idea.
5. Helps you find the most vulnerable point with which to close the sale – the key issue.
6. Gives the other party a feeling of importance. When you show you respect their opinion, they are more likely to respect yours.

Profiling for strategic level negotiation

Various forms of strategic negotiation analysis have been developed, and understanding this as a buyer or seller is critical. This typically comes into play when the negotiations are from a buyer with significant spend, who has a significant range of services and products that his or her organisation purchases. The buyer needs to understand the profile mix and negotiate differently in accordance with each supplier's place in that mix. The wise seller will be well aware of this and will seek to counter or have his own strategic response.

It soon becomes apparent that not all purchases are the same, for various compelling reasons. Some items are easy to source, easy to buy and have little relative impact on the company profit. Other items are notoriously difficult to source and buy. There may well be huge risk or exposure if the supply is stopped or diminished. There may be some items which have huge profit implications on the company. There is also the amount as a buyer you spend in various sectors: a large spend can lend itself to some form of leverage; a low spend on an important item or service presents a very different challenge altogether.

Definition

The question then arises, how can/should I respond strategically as a buyer or a seller? The answer starts with definition. And successful definition begins with questions using a scale of 1–10 where 10 is high and 1 is low.

1. How easy is this item to source?
2. How much risk is involved with supply problems on this item?
3. How significant is the spend on this item relative to our total spend?
4. What is the profit impact of this item relative to our company totals?

Once we have asked ourselves and answered these questions, there are many potential combinations. For simplicity I filter those four combinations into four generic profiles which are as follows.

Profile 1	Profile 2	Profile 3	Profile 4
low spend low risk low impact low significance	high spend low risk any impact high significance	high spend high risk high impact high significance	low spend high risk any impact high significance

Identify appropriate strategies and cost management techniques

Each profile warrants a different approach to be taken in defining your strategy and the technique needed to manage costs.

Profile 1

This is akin to commodity purchases. A good example would be individual items of stationery. Possible considerations for your strategy would include:

- **Introduce a blanket order/release process.**
- **Automate communications with suppliers, eg use an automated RFQ (request for quote) process or if your business is large enough consider EDI.**
- **Bundle similar items for larger consolidated purchases.**
- **Standardise specifications; standardise choice.**
- **Get purchasing personnel out of the execution loop.**
- **Minimise attention on the supplier or simply let it go.**

Profile 2

This has low profit impact but high market risk. A good example would be some kind of specialised bespoke CRM database linked with your accounting system. Possible considerations for your strategy would include:

- **Challenge or work on the specification.**
- **Seek alternatives that are more commonly available, eg off the shelf software.**
- **Double check the requirement: do we really need to restrict our choice like this?**
- **Challenge suppliers to develop generic equivalents.**
- **Consolidate with profile 3 items to improve leverage.**
- **Set targets for suppliers to keep prices under control.**
- **Find ways to enhance or improve the security of supply.**
- **Reduce the problem that created the need in the first place.**

Profile 3

This has a high profit impact and low market risk or difficulty. Practitioners often call this the 'leverage quadrant' because these items or services are easily sourced and any specification adjustment or CPR usually has a high impact on profit. Negotiating stances on these items can be robust. Possible considerations for your strategy would include:

- **Assure that buying is done on short-term deals.**
- **Unilaterally reject price increases.**
- **Challenge suppliers to provide discounts and rebates as a prerequisite for future business.**
- **Drive price year on year.**
- **Exhibit an expectant assertive CPR negotiation style.**
- **When price has been minimised, consider moving toward profile 4 on your terms in order to drive continuous improvement in cost, quality, etc.**

Profile 4

This has high profit impact and high market difficulty. This is a strategic purchase. A good example comes from my own world where we regularly contract with teams of high-quality, experienced tele-marketers. Because our reputation is based on the results, these relationships are highly strategic, very difficult to acquire and have a huge impact on our bottom line. Possible considerations for your strategy would include:

- **Manage the supplier by daily or weekly interventions.**
- **Seek mutual exclusivity for competitive advantage.**
- **Grow the relationship.**
- **Continuous improvement.**
- **Expand the supply market by fostering supplier development programs.**

- **Training others to acquire the skills and experience to become suppliers.**
- **Use open book costing.**
- **Seek and approve alternative sources.**
- **If supplier becomes complacent, introduce profile 3 tactics.**

If you are the seller in these settings, the buyers strategic options are areas of weakness which you need to actively consider and counter.

The authority of your counterpart

Ensure your counterpart has the authority to negotiate

Negotiation can only succeed between equals who both have the authority to agree on any of the decisions that will need to be reached. If either party – buyer or seller – does not have that authority, the negotiation cannot be concluded. It is important to understand what authority levels exist in your counterpart's company.

Part of the necessary questioning process is to establish the real authority of your counterpart and any team members he or she may introduce. As a general observation it should be obvious that both parties must have the authority and the determination to change the various components of an agreement. In other words, there is no value in getting to the bargaining phase only to find that your counterpart does not have the authority to agree on the tradeable variables.

The first question is, what title does my counterpart have? Does that title clearly establish their authority? Even if they are a senior partner or managing director you can check by asking the innocent question, 'Beside yourself, who else is involved in the decision-making process?'

Where our counterpart's title is less clear, we must check whether they have the authority that the negotiation requires. State, 'We are going to move to the final negotiation phase next Tuesday; can I take it that you have the authority to agree the final terms?', or better still, 'Who else in your organisation needs to be involved in agreeing the final terms?' If there is anyone else, make sure that they are there. One tactical tip here is to ask a question in a meeting, such as 'Will your company policy support this?', and then watch their eyes and observe who everyone looks at – that is nearly always the real decision maker or the prime influencer.

Check the power behind the scenes

Often there are influencers and powerful contributors behind the scenes. We must uncover who they are by asking W questions:

- **What other individuals are consulted before decisions are reached?**
- **Whose opinions help to set strategy, tactics and policy for our counterpart?**
- **Does the decision require an expert or technical specialist's approval?**
- **Who are those experts, and what is the extent of their influence?**

When we are pursuing this we should build a humanogram, a human map of who does what in the organisation. Get your counterpart to help you build it; let them draw on it with pencil or pen. You might even ask whether any of these individuals play sport together or socialise together, thus finding powerful pairings – which may be helpful information indeed.

Manage the power behind the scenes

During the preparation phase we should have uncovered the existence of these individuals and either found a way to negotiate them out of the process, or, more likely, insisted that we meet them at an early stage so that we can build our knowledge of the factors important to each one.

We then ask for an informal meeting with all of them present. We have met or telephoned each one individually beforehand. We make an informal presentation that takes into account all their individual requirements. During this informal presentation we ask each one in turn if all their requirements have been satisfied. When we are clear that they have, we either move into negotiation, or agree to reconvene with our counterpart, to conduct the negotiation proper.

If we have not covered all their requirements, simply take responsibility and control of the next step. You might say, 'John and Peter, I will come back to you first with some revised calculations. When we are sure we have agreed them, shall we all meet again one last time, say next Wednesday here at 2 pm?'

Have we got the decision maker/s?

Clearly it is very difficult, if not impossible, to get an order on the day if the decision maker is not there. For that reason, before you agree the visit, why not make it a habit to ask for all the decision-makers to be present. Try saying something similar to this: 'Who else besides yourself will be involved in making this decision? As the sales manager of Sercombe Engineering, you're a very busy person – and because I appreciate how valuable your time is, I'm going to get right down to business. I'm sure you'll appreciate my time is also valuable. So with this in mind, I'll explain all the facts of our service to you in explicit detail, and if you have any questions, I will be delighted to answer them. It's really important that the MD is there because if you feel this business-generating programme meets your needs and budget I expect you to tell me. On the other hand, if you feel as though it doesn't, please tell me that too, and I'll be on my way. However, I do expect you both to give me a decision that day. I'm sure you agree this is fair.'

If the decision maker is unable to make the meeting (which will happen from time to time), you might use some questions like these:

- **What other people will you consult about these ideas?**
- **Who else will have an impact on these ideas? What do you think their views might be?**
- **Will the board or buying committee form a decision based on somebody's recommendations? If so will it be yours? If not, then whose? Will you be recommending us? (If the answer is 'no', then handle the uncovered objections. If the answer is 'yes', then ask, 'Just to make sure I've done my job properly, can we go through the advantages of our solution as you see them? What are the main benefits as you view them?')**
- **Who else besides yourself will be involved in making this decision?**
- **What are the main benefits you see of our services that you'll discuss with the MD? (Get the prospect to relay the benefits and you gently correct or amplify them, eg 'You'll also want to mention xyz'.)**
- **It would help if I could be with you when you talk to the MD. Could you arrange that please?**

Discover the true decision maker

If you are in a group meeting with a potential client company, it is usually not difficult to discover who is the true authority or decision maker in the room: ask a question that can only be answered by a director or the equivalent, for example:

- **How does that square with your corporate policy?**
- **How will that reflect upon your financial targets for this year?**
- **Could this support your company acquisition programme?**
- **Could the implications of that have a bearing on your overall company strategy?**

Watch to whom everyone's eyes turn. This will be the most senior person in the room. If somebody else still elects to answer, they are probably the tactical decision maker for that project, so you should try and cultivate relations with them and the other party, who probably has the ultimate authority.

But how can you do this on the telephone, when such useful clues are not available? Ask the same questions! If the prospect fumbles, evades or is not decisively clear, they may be a junior. So ask, 'Who would have the ultimate say in authorising a decision like this?' Do not say, 'Who would allocate (or authorise) the budget for this?' You will find the decision maker is often not the person who controls the budget. For example, major in-house training programmes are usually authorised by a senior line manager or director (strategic role), but the training or personnel manager finds the budget and approves programme details (tactical role).

It is also likely there will be more than one decision maker. A friend of mine sells computer systems and his company recently got the Homebase account. They had to convince 14 decision makers before they finally got the order. On major sales it takes an average of five decision makers to close a sale, of which your rep may only have met two. So on such sales you may want to build a humanogram, a map of everyone in the decision-making chain.

14

Handling long-term negotiations

Longer term negotiations have their own peculiarities. They do still follow the PREPBAR© process but they will often need some specific thought and some specific responses. In this chapter I want to relate two recent stories and draw out some essential pointers that can help shape an informed approach to such deals.

Story 1

One of my colleagues is involved in a faith-based school, run by his local church. They have around 150 pupils and have property in the centre of their town. For five years or more the school has been keenly looking for land on which to build, or property that could be adapted. As with most UK towns, neither was readily available. The school had been steadily growing, was looking to expand and was very keen to find a solution.

Unexpectedly a commercial office building came onto the market in the summer of 2008, on a plot of land very close to the existing premises. Architects soon determined that with some care, it would be possible to adapt the building and the land, to give the space the school needed. The property came onto the market because of the recession. Not long before, a deal had been lined up with a developer, and that deal had fallen through because of the recession. My colleague made the initial approach.

The negotiation was an open bidding process with gradually escalating bids. Working with his trusted local commercial agent, together they agreed an offer price which was acceptable to the school. No formal valuation was commissioned, but a structural survey was completed as concern had been expressed about some of the building's structures.

An informal valuation from the commercial property agent had been provided, taking into account the state of the building. One of the difficulties was that there were two sellers involved. The freehold land owned by a neighbouring organisation (a charitable trust) and the building leasehold owned by a property company. In this first round, the school was outbid by a local housing association who wanted to demolish and create flats. The school was clear, yes they need the land and that was a well known fact, but equally because of the charitable status, and limitations on funds, the school could not afford to get into a bidding war. Final bids were in by September and by October the school was informed they had lost the deal. The option to rebid was offered but the school stuck to its position and the deal was lost.

Over the next few months the housing association ran out of money and pulled out of the deal. In spring 2009 it was back on the market and the school made an offer four per cent less than the previous offer. Not to be outdone the housing association surprised all the parties with a totally new kind of offer. This offer was slightly higher than the school's but required the sellers to accept 25 per cent down and the rest in one year's time.

By asking appropriate questions the school discovered that the sellers needed to move quickly, and as a result the school agreed the deal. The price was inclusive of both land and building and the school negotiated a one month exclusivity deal which conditioned both parties to expedite the deal to completion within one month.

It was at this point that a previously unforeseen problem emerged; the joy of dealing with two sellers. One seller was governed by a set of trustees who were at a distance geographically. This proved to cause delays as different details went back and forth. United Kingdom trust law forces trustees to get the best possible deal at the time of the deal, so a revaluation of the land was commissioned out of perceived legal obligation. This in turn caused the two sellers to face a renegotiation around the split of the price. The split got renegotiated in the middle of the negotiations and significantly affected the length of time being taken. Six months or more were added to the time frame by this unexpected process.

Another unexpected surprise caused further delays. One of the sellers, as we have stated already, had a board of trustees, and instead of reviewing the whole document they dealt with one point at a time. So for example it seemed that they would read the contract, get to one point of contention and haggle over that single point rather than looking at the whole contract producing one list and then addressing all the points in one go. The net outcome for my colleague was huge delay that was unhelpful, untimely and costly. The first point of contention would be hammered out, then two months later another issue would be raised.

The challenge in a situation like this is to maintain goodwill and yet keep up appropriate pressure or momentum. A balance between patience and pushing. To achieve this balance, regular personal communication through one designated individual was maintained. This was done personally with individuals from both sellers not just the lawyers.

The school subsequently negotiated a £10,000 reduction because of the delays and extra costs. The school also intelligently used trust law to speed the process. They made it clear, as they were approaching what appeared to be the final conclusion of the deal, that if the deal was not concluded within 'x' weeks they would have to renegotiate the price. Essentially what they were arguing was that the same trust law used by the seller to increase their split would have to be invoked by the school. In other words to comply with the law's requirement to get the best possible deal at the time of the deal, the offer price could not be sustained if the negotiation was going to carry on any longer. The sellers responded with uncharacteristic speed!

Lessons learned

In essence the school has negotiated well, but a checklist built from experience would help in any future negotiation:

1. What information is in the public domain and how do we manage that? The local community was well aware of the school's urgent need for more space. The school could not hide that fact so had to be clear on its highest price and make it clear it would not entertain a bidding war.
2. What legal implications are there for us and our counterpart? A bit of research here, would have thrown up the charitable trust status and this could have been talked through openly at the outset and delays negotiated away. I would encourage a thorough dialogue on this issue in every substantial negotiation. List every possible implication of a legal nature and develop a simple strategy to handle every issue expediently.
3. Who are the real decision makers and what are the implications? The reality here was that two very independent organisations were jointly involved. One commercially driven, and the other constrained by trust law. With the value of hindsight, sitting down with the individuals involved – even attending a trustees meeting – could have clarified the implications of the processes involved. With a bit of good will a more efficient quicker approach by all parties to the issues involved could have been mutually beneficial.
4. Ask 'What if?' at several stages especially related to timing. Here the exclusive deal for one month blinded my colleague a little to the potential causes and subsequent

ramifications of time-related issues. It is wise to ask ourselves how realistic is this purported time frame? What could possibly slow it down and how could we address that?

Story 2

A small group of friends owned four fields in a South Western country town purchased together partly for lifestyle reasons, and partly as a retirement-planning asset. Some eighteen months back, out of the blue they were approached to see if there would be any interest in selling that land or at least part of it. The initial approach was made by a solicitor who mailed an invitation for an exploratory meeting with the key individual from a community project that needed new land in order to relocate, and subsequently move some or all of their facilities. At the meeting it became clear that his objective was to ask if the group would be willing to consider parting with the land.

The first response from the group was to approach a land agent to get a feel for the likely values involved, likely costs of the process, and the key issues that might arise. This agent was involved at the first meeting with the potential buyer and helped craft some of the key questions that needed to be asked.

Subsequently with some further research a new, more experienced local land agent was commissioned and helped in a variety of ways to walk the land with the group of owners, and discuss the various configurations the land could be sold in. From the group's perspective the idea was to make sure they were wise in how some of the land should be sold and in particular to ensure that the remaining land (approximately half the total) would potentially be able to increase in value as a result of the development, rather than decrease in value.

From a total of four fields, two were selected and the group, together with the land agent, met with the potential buyer and their land advisor, with a clear goal of, among other things, exploring in depth his motivations and his needs, and gauging his negotiation style. In their minds one question all the group members wanted answered was, 'Can we trust what he says?'

From this meeting, the group discovered that the buyer was passionate about local community projects and a bit of an expert in driving through such projects to completion, including planning issues and funding. He made some suggestions himself about the remaining land which were duly noted and subsequently checked out.

The land agent acting for the group put in writing his best estimation of the likely value of the land for recreational use and many different options were explored including: renting, leasing, selling, who owns what roads, and who pays for the roads. The group asked him to meet with the buyer with instructions and came up with a figure finally agreed, subject to planning and other important stipulations that the group needed to have included.

One of the potential danger points was that the four fields had been sold to the group by two different landowners. In British law there is commonly a covenant on land that is sold, which means that if the new owners sell within 20 years, they must pay an agreed percentage of the additional value of that land to the original landowners. This nasty piece of contractual law is commonly known as the uplift clause.

A key negotiation process then began to get the former landowners to agree a sensible uplift value, otherwise the whole process would be put in jeopardy. Added to this was the potential future value of the land that remained, and the group's intent was therefore to negotiate a deal where a one-off payment would release them from any future uplift implications.

The two previous owners were very different in style and negotiation attitude, so a decision was made to focus on the toughest of the two first, and then when agreement was reached, to use the progress made with that first negotiation to set firm expectations for the second.

At the first negotiation, the group chose to take the potential buyer with them. The logic was that his passion for the local community, and his non-commercial desire for good, would help set realistic expectations and thus prevent the uplift clause from sinking the whole process. The process worked and terms were agreed to be incorporated into the contracts, subject to planning, with both parties.

Lessons and considerations

In the main a great outcome, a true win–win–win. The group got the deal they wanted with an enhanced future outcome. The community project got its land in a perfect location, and the two previous landowners got a reasonable amount which would have been lost altogether if their demands had been too much for the project to succeed.

The group followed PREPBAR© to the letter, so let's take a look at some of the implications:

1. Patience. From the outset the group knew they had to be seen to be reluctant and not in a rush. Partly because of the obvious impact of that on the pricing expectations of the buyer, and also from experience, they knew it would take time, and lots of it. Every time they talked together they encouraged each other to be slower than they wanted; not rushing any correspondence, phone call, or response. This took huge discipline as it worked against the natural instincts – the 'get it done now' qualities that the individuals in the group possessed.
2. Knowing what you want. At the outset the group of four met and thrashed through every potential response from no sale at all to selling all the land. They spent time working with each other until they were all crystal clear on exactly what they each wanted so there would be no weak link in any meeting. Total unity gave them strength in their chosen position.

   One of the key issues was knowing what they wanted for their future, and ensuring they protected that future. They agreed to negotiate a short-term deal that was good, in return for a long-term deal that was much more substantial, holding even greater potential. The group also chose one spokesman, the point person who acted on their behalf. At every point the group discussed the precise manner in which the spokesman would act, and agreed the potential alternatives. On every occasion the spokesman went in strongly prepared and with the full weight of the group's support behind him. There was not a single meeting or conversation in which he felt unprepared or weak. That was a significant achievement.

3. Choosing the right expert. It was clear that with issues of valuation, land law and the inevitable potential hidden dangers and possibilities, an expert needed to be consulted early on. Both agents were good. The subsequent choice of the second agent came from a review meeting the group held, where greater experience and someone with that experience locally was deemed an important asset needed on the team.
4. Understanding the buyer. Great care was taken preparing for meetings with the buyer. Local people were sounded out (a great place for social media as explained in Chapter 18). The group needed to know about his character, and his relevant history, and how much of what he said could be relied upon. In order to do this well at the plan and prepare stage, the agent was involved and a list of carefully crafted questions was produced and used in the interaction.
5. Aiming higher than you think. The uplift issue was trying; an irritant in what could have otherwise been a straightforward process. One person in the group was selected for the negotiations and those negotiations were meticulously prepared for with all the options and counter options discussed. The approach was agreed and began with a vastly reduced proposal. The key for the group here was agreeing a number and not being intimidated by it, seeing it as part of the whole process, and getting it dealt with early on.

15

Post-purchase remorse can undo the close

Needless to say, a cancelled sale or a non-payment does not constitute a sale. Just before Christmas I ordered a full-size pool table for the family. I had to wait 10 days for delivery and I began to have second thoughts. Would it be too big? Would it look really ugly? Would the family really use it? Was the supplier reputable? I began to feel so negative that I very nearly rang to cancel the order.

If I had cancelled, what would I have felt? I would have felt relief. Why? Because I would have removed the fear of loss. At the heart of non-renewal, cancellations and most customer care problems lies the fear of loss.

Let me put to you a little scenario. Suppose I said you have five minutes to make a phone call to your bank and you are allowed to instruct them to do only one of two things. You can instruct them to stop an investment going through which you now absolutely know will lose you £10,000 or you can instruct them to make an investment which you know, with equal certainty, will gain you £10,000. You can only give one of these instructions. I suspect that we would tell them to block the transaction that was going to lose money, though the net result would be the same either way. The fear of loss is many times more powerful than the appeal of gain.

This is exactly the dilemma your customer has when you ask them to sign the order. They fear that your product or service will not perform, or there will be problems up the road, or their boss will criticise them, or their people will not accept it. They know they can probably sue you if there is an outright breach of contract, but that is not the worry. You might consume their people's time, waste their materials, perhaps damage their relations with their own customers. The contingent risk is enormous.

That fear is in their minds even if the transaction is small. Suppose the contract opportunities, the renewal or the ad doesn't work? It is often easier to stay with the devil they know, despite the pain, than risk more pain with a new product or supplier. Marketers refer to this as 'post-purchase remorse'. In this context it is important to remember that the *fear of loss nearly always exceeds the appeal of gain*.

As a seller we conclude the negotiation and we feel great, but what do our buyers feel? What do they feel while they are waiting? What do they feel when the invoice arrives? What do they feel when the faxed leads drop on their desk? I suggest that for many of our subscribers this is one of the most potentially dangerous moments in our relationship with them. They will often feel twinges of disappointment and if we do nothing for them here, I am sure that the seeds of cancellation are already sown. Some of them will feel literal fear – fear of loss, fear that they have made a mistake. Some are very definitely afraid of the process involved or overwhelmed by the thought of it. What should be a pleasant moment, a magic moment, is anything but that – often in reality it is a very negative moment. It is at this moment that the salesperson, the one the buyer trusted this decision to, is silent and non-existent. The only person the buyer is likely to have meaningful contact with is the accounts department chasing for money, which is more than likely going to compound the fear or anxiety.

What should be done at this time? The ideal would be to have someone give:

- **genuine personal contact;**
- **confidence in the product;**
- **belief that this will work for the customer;**
- **motivation to use the product.**

And also to:

- **remove the fear of loss;**
- **stimulate the appeal of gain.**

Most sellers conducting field sales have in the region of six to eight sales per month – hopefully more after reading this book. A little thank-you note would go a long way to overcoming the buyer's fears and requires little effort from the seller. When is the last time a salesperson told you how much he or she really appreciated your business, or for that matter even thanked you?

Keeping positive passion for your service and product range is essential for the close

Another step towards making your negotiations successful is to make the products or services you sell a passion. If we are not passionate about the product, it will be hard for anyone else to like it. A passion for the product is more contagious than any disease; it will spread to others and impact the outcome of negotiations.

In our negotiations we already know that we should price our product or service well to ensure that the customer perceives our total package or offering is value for money. Our passion is critical here too. If we do not have a passion for the product, the customer will never be convinced of its value. If we have passion, the chance of the buyer having a positive assessment is also high. In pricing there should be an element of what we should get and also the value the customer gets. If the customer comes to have a passion for the product, perceiving it to be good value, then renewals or repeat business click more easily into place.

Martin Shafiroff believes strongly in having conviction. He states, 'all great business successes have strong convictions in what they are doing. Essentially the first person you must sell to, if you want to succeed, is yourself. This is vital. When you believe in what you are doing, the other party evaluating your comments is going to react accordingly.' What Shafiroff believes is that it is only when you have these strong convictions that you can superimpose your beliefs on others. In fact he believes that a salesperson's convictions are so powerful that even when he or she sells or follows up on the telephone, the seller's convictions can be sensed by the other party.

Conviction comes when salespeople believe so strongly in the value of the product that their single driving motivation is to provide value for their customers. In fact the best salespeople are more anxious to provide benefits to their customers than they are to earn fat commissions. When money is the primary driving force, salespeople rarely succeed because prospects see £ signs in their eyes. Business is negotiated well when you really believe in the interest of the customer and that your product or service is the best value of its kind. Buyers, you should be passionate too about your company, department, products and services. This increases the perceived value and worth of the transaction to your sales counterpart.

16

Tough or effective?

Characteristics of effective negotiators

Being tough is not the same as being effective. Often, being tough leads to immovable positions that create negative feelings and more frequently lead to negotiations that are deadlocked. The source of the toughness usually lies in incompetence or insecurity. Applying some of the keys we have shared together will build your competence.

Effective negotiators will have the following attributes:

- **They know their ideal and work patiently and consistently for it.**
- **They can be tough if – and only if – that would be productive.**
- **They are very slow and rather mean in giving concessions.**
- **They are not frightened by the thought of deadlock.**
- **They never make it seem they have 'won' a point.**

- **They always prepare their information and think through the possible obstacles.**
- **They always rehearse the approach.**

Effective negotiators look at buying and selling in the same deal

One of my clients sells PCs and software. They recently negotiated the biggest deal ever in their 14-year history. The contract was to supply PCs and services across Europe. First they looked for a way to earn authority by choosing to take on a small deal worth just a few thousand pounds. They saw the potential not in the job but in the customer. Price was stated to be a key issue, so they enhanced their credibility by going back through the supply chain. The customer wanted extra discount; my client insisted that for an increased discount of 1.5 per cent the order should be increased from 45 to 70 units. The discount didn't cost him; it actually gained him more profit on the whole deal. Because of the discount the customer then discovered some unused end-of-year budget and placed a further £100,000 worth of orders.

My client asked for payment on delivery and got it! In turn, they negotiated 60 days' payment terms from their supplier. They now had the additional benefit of several hundred thousand pounds earning interest for 60 days.

In the purchasing process they went first to distributors and evaluated the distributors on the basis of a similar quote for 40 machines. They tested on interest shown, speed of response, and hunger.

Having decided which distributor they preferred, they then went direct to the manufacturer and negotiated a few extra percentage points. They discussed other ways in which they could improve their margins. The end result was a pleased customer, a happy distributor, a willing and cooperative manufacturer, and a much richer client. They looked at both sides of the negotiating equation.

Effective negotiators balance their team carefully

There may well be occasional, or more frequent, times when the negotiation requires more than one person on your team. It may be superiors. It may be technical experts. Whoever is involved there must be clear ground rules:

- **You are responsible.**
- **That means you have the authority on the day. Your MD or manager must make that clear and be there in a supporting role.**
- **Other team members know that they defer to you. You have set clear parameters of what they can and cannot say, and when they can say it.**
- **They know that they only contribute when drawn in by you.**
- **You summarise at every stage of agreement.**
- **You agree the final deal – after which they shut up!**

If you are wise, you will have rehearsed the possible outcomes with your team. Let them know where their danger points occur. Your counterpart should not have more people than you, nor should they have experts present in fields that you do not.

Effective negotiators keep the whole package in mind

Above all, effective negotiators have trained themselves to avoid the ever-open trap of price preoccupation. They keep the whole proposal in mind all the time, and keep it in their counterpart's thinking all the time as well.

The whole package includes:

- **the product or service itself;**
- **particular functions or attributes;**
- **the benefits of those functions or attributes;**
- **the overall benefit or gain of using or investing in the service;**
- **the positive or negative impact of publicity surrounding their company or product range;**
- **quantity;**
- **delivery;**
- **payment options;**
- **clearance of existing stocks;**
- **maintenance and service;**
- **price and profit.**

Price is last, because in their mind it is just one of many potential ingredients and not the pivotal point of the agreement. In the process of keeping the whole deal in mind they will ask for all concerns and all objections when any single point is raised. They will then say, 'Can I now take it that those represent all your concerns?'

One of my associates was trying to negotiate an increase in his daily fee of five per cent from a long-term client who had been using our staff for nearly three years (one day per week). The client was important to him and was understandably reluctant to pay more.

My colleague thought through the whole package and came up with a solution that delighted the client, but gave him not five per cent but around 20 per cent! How did he do it? He reduced his daily fee by £30, and asked in return for £75 commission for every tender enquiry generated. My colleague was totally safe, knowing he would average more than one tender enquiry per day worked, thus yielding him an average increase of 20 per cent. The client was delighted because the fee was now performance related. All that, simply by keeping the whole deal in mind.

Effective negotiators have a good alternative

If you have no alternative to this particular negotiated agreement, you are weakened and constrained. The effective negotiator understands this clearly and endeavours to have a good fallback position.

Fallback in this sense means the best alternative course of action open to you if this negotiation fails completely. It can make all the difference to where the power balance will settle. The stronger your option here, the less you will feel the need to make concessions. Equally, the more confidence you will have in making demands of the other side.

Where they have it, effective negotiators will make sure that their counterpart understands their strength. Where they don't have it, they will not give that fact away!

Effective negotiators avoid irritators

It is fairly obvious what irritators are! Things that irritate your counterpart. They would include the following:

- **unpleasant personal habits;**
- **an over-friendly or familiar approach when the relationship is not genuinely at that level;**
- **bad or inappropriate language;**
- **smoking – never light up unless your counterpart has;**
- **embarrassing others who make mistakes in the negotiation process;**
- **voicing personal opinions about others – they nearly always backfire;**
- **being greedy;**

- **adopting a triumphant manner;**
- **annoying phrases – particularly ones that appear patronising or smutty.**

If you don't know whether you are guilty of any of these, ask a colleague whose judgement and motives you trust to point them out. An ancient proverb says, 'Faithful are the wounds of a friend.' In other words, better the marginal embarrassment of a friend's observation, rather than poor performance and potential alienation in the negotiation process.

One particular irritator is a consistent and apparently mean approach to negotiating – where you keep asking – in a long-term relationship. A good example would be if you had a restaurant that you and your family liked to use either regularly or from time to time. If you ask for a deal each time you go, you probably irritate some members of your family and you will irritate the proprietor because of your constant asking. It appears mean. Far better here to sit down with the proprietor and agree a long-term arrangement that leaves him or her motivated and gives you the deal you are looking for.

I made this mistake with my plumber. We have a fairly large home and the heating system needs urgent attention several times each year. Every time I used him he would give me excellent service – even mobile phone support out of hours – but it seemed to him that I would always haggle. In the end it irritated him and he lost the will to service me. I had made the mistake of gaining in the short term and losing out in the longer term.

Effective negotiators embrace mistakes

One of my friends has a quotation that he wants on his tombstone: 'Where there is no ox the stall is clean, but much strength comes by the ox.' If you want the strength of the ox, then you will have to put up with a bit of muck from time to time. Mistakes are the fertiliser of success. We don't much like the constituent components of fertiliser. They smell, they are unpleasant, but they do bring growth.

Mistakes in negotiation are inevitable. In this book I have deliberately quoted personal examples of where I have got it wrong. That's because it's not that abnormal. We are not omnipotent – thank God! We cannot possibly win every single situation. But when we get it wrong there is a simple choice: do we resent the experience as an intruder or welcome it as a friend?

Every mistake I have related in this book has taught me something. Sometimes I get uptight but mostly I am grateful – it is another building block in the process of aspiring to be an effective negotiator.

Effective negotiators have an eye for body language

I don't overrate this skill. There is a great deal of complexity about body language, so much so that in my experience, training in depth rarely helps, because of that complexity. In other words, there is so much to learn and remember that negotiators rarely use it effectively. And it is not a perfect science; there are different interpretations for the same body movements.

There are some simple applications, however, and the effective negotiator has learnt them. The classic ploy of some negotiators is to sit their counterpart in a chair that is lower. It can very easily make you feel less important, less confident, and it is a ploy to watch out for. The same negotiators may well position your chair in a disadvantageous manner. They may have it a long way away, or at an awkward angle. Your response is simple. If you don't like the chair – simply say, 'I am uncomfortable, do you mind if I stand?' If you don't like the placement of the chair, move it with confidence and say, 'I would like to move closer if that is OK.'

Avoid sitting down in reception. You are nearly always offered low, uncomfortable chairs that do not prepare you properly for the negotiation ahead. I always stand up and walk around even in the smallest of reception areas. The reason is that the receptionist cannot forget me and will do her best to get me to my appointment. I feel confident, in control, and consequently build my authority. In the process I read their brochures, look at certificates and read their in-house newsletters. I have more information.

Watch out for significant movement at critical moments in the negotiation process. I was retained by a Swedish printer to negotiate a large printing contract worth in the region of £1.25 million. When we were in the final stages of negotiation I went through the proposed pricing structure, expecting resistance. But at that point the buyer jumped up and in animated fashion started walking up and down. The price was in fact a very pleasant surprise, and he could hardly contain his emotion. It told me that I could have asked for more. It gave me a very strong position when it came to trading concessions.

Tightly folded arms at the start of the negotiation and again at the beginning of the bargaining phase are normal indicators of mild stress or intensity. Don't worry about them, but do watch for the moment when those arms relax and slide onto the table or on to their lap. They are relaxing, and you can be increasingly confident that your requests are acceptable – there is probably a positive disposition towards your approach.

Watch out for a negative shift. Negative shifts can include 'wandering eyes', meaning that they will not look you in the face. Irritated breathing sounds, tapping fingers, leaning back over-casually in the chair, an apathetic air – all these are normal signs that you have lost their interest or that they have made up their mind not to agree. You can still recover from this position with your statement-question, for example: 'Something does not appear totally clear here. Can I ask, what are your feelings about the total agreement at this point?'

Effective negotiators always stay in control

Staying in control at every stage of the negotiation is our responsibility. It is our job to get the best deal for us while helping our counterpart to feel that they have a good deal themselves. The only way we can do that is by staying in control:

- **Set the agenda. That means you determine when the meeting takes place, where, and what the items on the agenda are.**
- **Type the agenda and send, fax or e-mail it.**
- **Take control of the meeting itself. Start by going through the agenda and agreeing the process for that particular meeting.**
- **Lead each step of the meeting – following the six elements of negotiation.**
- **Summarise every point of agreement along the way.**
- **Summarise the final agreement.**
- **Put it all in writing.**

If the negotiation is getting bogged down in trivial detail or if it is going off track, you must assert control. You can do this by bringing the conversation back on track with 'I've been wondering whether?' and then move straight into the statement-question.

Characteristics of ineffective negotiators

Ineffective negotiators are never sure of what the right move is or isn't. They will generally not prepare and not take the process seriously.

Ineffective negotiators will show the following characteristics:

- **no preparation;**
- **no rehearsal;**
- **no commitment to the overall objectives or the negotiation in hand;**
- **insecurity and uncertainty in their opening position;**
- **do not have or inspire confidence in their requests or proposals;**
- **frequently succumb to price-rotting pressure placed on them;**
- **often get bogged down in the trivial and will trivialise the important.**

17

Dos and don'ts

This chapter contains a number of practical points or easily absorbed summaries of skills or attributes that can be quickly acquired.

Do always maintain the initiative

This is one of the golden rules. If you don't maintain the initiative, you will lose three things. First, *money*. You have spent money leading up to this moment. If you throw away the initiative now it will be wasted. Second, *control*. By applying your skills you will have generated a certain momentum; the negotiation should be moving, and moving in your direction. The moment you lose the initiative you have lost that control; you will bring the negotiation to a grinding halt and both your counterpart's interests and yours will be lost. The third and most damaging thing you will lose is *business*. As you well know, not all negotiations are finally concluded when we meet. In fact in one recent survey, 50 per cent of sales negotiations were not concluded within six months. Things crop up, changes occur and we must be ready for those eventualities.

Maintaining the initiative means you predetermine the next point of contact and take responsibility for it. You will finish any conversation or any phase of the process with a closing sentence that predetermines the next point of action. 'As promised, I will make a point of contacting you next Tuesday to agree our next meeting.' You make a similar statement in your confirming letter. Agree the next step if more than one meeting is likely to be necessary. You take the initiative in the first place and you don't give it back.

Do put things in writing

Putting things in writing is so important. It helps you to keep authority and control. It avoids all kinds of embarrassing mistakes, and often helps to clarify issues that would otherwise be clouded.

Five points about writing:

- **Put any agreement in writing. Wherever possible, volunteer to write the agreement or contract.**
- **Write down all key points during the bargaining process. Be highly visible in the process. When it suits you, show them to your counterpart and agree those points together.**
- **Write the agenda before you meet. If it is a group meeting, we should write the agenda after we have made contact with each person, to ensure that they feel represented. Make sure you then send a copy to each individual. Remember, what is written has authority. So think through what you could carry into the negotiation with you, in the form of written statements or proposals. In many situations we can win the advantage by carrying written evidence to support our opening offer.**

- **Use customer or supplier statements in typed form, to add weight to any particular point you may be making. In particular, use them to back up any claims of advantage or benefit that you may be making during the bargaining phase.**
- **Written points should be on file in the event of contractual problems later.**

Do learn to use higher authority

In a negotiation it may help us if we have limited authority. What we can give away is minimised. 'I need to discuss that with my MD', or 'with my partner', or 'with my department manager'. You can make a company policy that actually reinforces the fact. In other words, if you wish, you can actually make it company policy that your authority is limited in certain situations and you must therefore refer to whoever is stipulated as the authority.

In real terms, don't go beyond your own authority. If you are reaching a point in the negotiation where you are being asked to agree terms for which you do not have the authority, use a phrase like this: 'I am authorised to negotiate within certain parameters. I can take this one back to my MD, I doubt if he will agree. But what if we could...'

Do know the boundaries of authority within which your counterpart operates. Make sure you know what they can and cannot agree. Otherwise you may trade a concession unnecessarily.

Where it helps, insist on speaking to a higher authority in your counterpart's organisation. A friend of mine was negotiating a price from his insurance company. He selected a policy from a company offering a special deal for a second car. He was refused because of a minor accident three years earlier. He would not take no for an answer. He patiently elevated the issue through two levels of management before finding the individual to whom the gain or loss of the business really mattered, when he finally secured his deal. The result for him was a real saving of £300 pa. The lesson learnt was to escalate the process and use higher authority to get the result he wanted.

Do conceal your emotions

Emotions – including body language – are like words: the more you express them, the more you give away. Try to keep a straight face that gives away nothing in particular. Avoid obvious expressions of relief or elation or panic! Anything you give away here will give clues to your counterpart.

You can of course try to use emotion or body language deliberately as a smokescreen. The problem here is that it is difficult to maintain the act, and sooner or later you are likely to be found out. The moment that happens, you will have generated some distrust. Your own standing and authority will be significantly weakened and your integrity questioned – rightly so.

Do ask for discount when paying cash

As a general rule, ask for more and you will get more. If you are paying by credit card there is always a surcharge for the person supplying you, anything from three to five per cent. Make a habit of asking for discount – say, 'I understand that the credit card costs you five per cent; if I pay by cash, I assume that I can knock that off the bill.'

It won't work all the time because there are some people who actually prefer the lower risk of having less cash and you will have to find another approach. But do try it anyway.

Do use experts

There are times when it can be beneficial to use other people who have particular skills. If you are buying print and promotion, you can read the next chapter. Or you could call a company specialising in cost reduction.

I am retained from time to time to lead a team in a negotiation where the stakes are high, or to act as the sole negotiator where the order or supply value is high relative to other transactions that a company may make. Sometimes clients will just use me to help them prepare and rehearse. When the deal is important or valuable, it makes sense to call in a professional.

It always makes sense to have everyone in a negotiation role trained. The smallest of skill improvements can make a difference of 10 per cent or more to your bottom line. I was involved in a seminar recently. The following week, three people who had put some of the material into practice were already reaping rewards after just seven days. One of them had negotiated over £50,000 worth of new business. One of the others had totally revised his presentation and gone in at twice the price he originally intended. The third person had always been apprehensive about the negotiating process. She discovered a new confidence and was already trying it out. There are hundreds of testimonials of individuals who have quickly saved over 10 per cent on all their buying activity.

If you regularly use hotels, there are specialists who do nothing else but negotiate special deals for customers. They charge you nothing and earn their income from the hotel-paid commission. It may just save you time and give you a better deal.

Don't expect to win them all

Negotiation can be discouraging. We can make some silly

mistakes, some unnecessary comments and we lose it. Either the deal does not get concluded, or our counterpart walks away with the better deal. Often, large amounts of energy, time and resource have been expended. The process can be so wearing at times.

Where you can, laugh! Reflect on something funny or absurd. Don't take it all too seriously. Ask yourself what you can learn, write it down and then apply the knowledge you have gained. Do remain enthusiastic. Business people need to maintain enthusiasm. Negotiation will always wear us down, wear down our aspirations; we need to keep positive.

Often your counterpart will react negatively in the negotiation. Expect it; don't be threatened or worn down by it. It is simply part of their attempt to lower your aspirations. Keep positive.

By the way, just in case you are wondering, I don't spend my entire life negotiating on everything. It can actually be embarrassing to friends and family and it can become unnecessarily stressful, particularly on small things. But I do make sure that on the major areas of expenditure I do at the very least think through the negotiation implications. Sometimes, because of the frenetic pace of life we will not take the time to negotiate on smaller areas of expenditure, and that can be a totally valid judgement to make. Equally, I try to be very careful to use my negotiation with small businesses and struggling companies to help them win.

Don't be afraid to break off negotiation

Don't be afraid to *break off negotiation for any reason* that you believe is legitimate. If you believe that the discussion is heading in a damaging direction, or if the unexpected arises and catches you by surprise – take a break. If you are leading a team, ask for time to confer privately. If you are on your own, take a short break or agree another meeting. Ask questions before you leave to ensure that you have covered and understood all the ground.

You should never be put under pressure to sign in haste. If you are being subjected to that, then break for your own reasons. You might say, 'There are one or two points I need to go away and consider more carefully; perhaps we can arrange to meet again next week', or 'I would like a fresh air break; please excuse me for 30 minutes.'

Never be put under pressure to sign during or after hospitality – particularly long lunches. Use those experiences legitimately to cement relationships, not to manipulate the deal. When travelling long distances, particularly by air, leave time before the negotiation. With transatlantic deals, never agree them on the day of travel. Dehydration and jet lag have real impact on your mind and body. You are almost certain to agree a poor deal if you settle it on the day of travel.

Don't attack your counterpart – attack the problem

Do separate the people from the negotiation. We need to support people, and attack the problem. Understand, use phrases like 'We really want the business to go through', then attack the problem.

There is a five-step process that can help us if we encounter some sticky personal problem or confrontation during the negotiation dialogue:

1. *Listen* to deflate. Often, when confrontation arises, the other person's emotions intensify. If we react to them we will allow the hot air of emotion to inflate the issue beyond its real size and importance.
2. *Sympathise* or empathise, and confirm the details. You might say, 'I think I understand, and if I were in your shoes I would probably feel the same. From what you are saying, the problem could be summarised like this... Did I get that

right?' Now the tension is defused, and we are ready once again to move forward. We have identified ourselves with their feelings and made it clear that it is quite all right to feel that way.

3. *Formulate* and offer a proposed solution. Or respond with an approach of a specific trading suggestion: 'If you... then we...'
4. *Action* any agreement made – be responsible for it.
5. *Confirm* any details verbally and then be seen to write them down.

Avoid reacting to confrontation or sensitive moments. That way you will avoid attacking individuals. Where you can, try to avoid jumping to self-defence. When in that position, never use inflammatory phrases like 'You let me down.' Instead, use phrases like 'I feel let down.' The five-step process will produce facts rather than feelings and cooperation rather than confrontation.

Your counterpart will almost certainly dislike the tension of these moments. They can be quite unnerving. Try to produce an environment in which you support each other and you jointly attack any real or perceived problem.

Don't show triumph

Don't show triumph. It creates resentment. It implies I won, and they lost. Be careful who you talk to, and what you say. The more you say, the more danger there is.

Any expression of elation will be interpreted negatively by your counterpart. They may begin to rue the deal and look for a way out. Be careful what you say to them, their staff or your staff. Pride goes before a fall, and that is eminently applicable here. The maxim to follow is 'Sign up then shut up.'

Don't deal in round numbers

If you are in consulting or training, round numbers are expected and the norm. But for the rest of us, round numbers cry out for attention. They shout out, 'I am designed to negotiate.' Typical round numbers would be £5, £10, £100, £1,000, £10,000, £100,000. There is a built-in incredibility. It will weaken your position from the beginning because your counterpart will automatically expect you to concede on price. It is saying as clearly as if you put it into words, 'I don't expect to get the figure mentioned here'!

Don't indicate movement before you need to

Don't signal willingness to move unless you want to. 'About', 'near', 'roughly' are words to avoid. They are words that spell movement or concession. They reveal that you are already willing to move. The phrase 'or near offer' is deadly. It is not a successful tactic for moving a deal forward; it is a concession, for nothing in return, and should never be used.

In fact these words have actually become your first concession and they are offering price as the legitimate first target for your counterpart. By your own action you have removed the defensive shield from your price.

Don't dig your heels in

Remember to focus on the overall interest. Don't take an intransigent position. Don't allow one element or one feature or one particular position to obscure the overall interest. Keep talking about that general interest. Keep the whole deal in mind, get their entire shopping list. Use a phrase like 'What other points did you want to discuss?', or 'What are the other issues that are important to you?'

If you dig your heels in on one particular issue, the chances are that push will become shove and you will end up with breakdown or deadlock. Sometimes the intransigent position is a reflection of greed. That smells as rotten as any bad fish, and your counterpart will rightly turn up their nose at it!

Don't be afraid to go back and try again

I shall never forget it. I was unintentionally eavesdropping in the club lounge at Heathrow and could not believe my luck! Next to me on the phone was a professional negotiator doing his stuff. Why would I be excited? Because you very rarely get to hear other professionals. This one was special. He negotiated the sale of aircraft and he had just been told he had lost a particular deal, which he had thought was in the bag.

For 20 minutes or so I listened to this consummate professional asking 'W' questions. He found out how many aircraft they were finally going to buy and how much they had agreed to pay. He discovered who they had agreed it with, what the spares and maintenance agreement was. He uncovered all the terms and conditions. He discovered what negotiable variables his competitor had used, and even though he had been given a firm thumbs-down he didn't give up. While I was still sitting there he had agreed a re-negotiation meeting.

When about to give up, ask yourself, 'What is wrong with one last try?'

Don't be afraid of risk

Negotiation is risky; the only thing that is more risky is not to negotiate. You may well get it wrong, wholly or in part.

When you are negotiating, be more willing to take risks and be seen to be willing; it implies confidence and will often pay off. Your counterpart will intuitively sense confidence in your approach and it will add to your authority.

Be quick to point out to your counterpart some of the risks they may be taking if they deal with another company. If you are the buyer, point out to your supplier some of the riskier elements of other potential buyers, stressing the risk-free environment that you may well be offering: your financial security, your commitment to expansion, your supplier payment record terms, etc.

If you are the seller, point out the security or guarantee of the MDSA© you offer. Show them that the absence of these attributes from other suppliers renders them vulnerable to risk. Try to quantify that risk with facts, figures, amounts and savings. Use a guarantee to eliminate the fear of risk. Deal effectively with risks your counterpart perceives, even if those risks don't really exist.

Don't succumb to dangerous phrases

Our counterpart may well have a stockpile of dangerous phrases, which include the following:

- **'You scratch my back and I'll scratch yours.' Loosely interpreted, it means, 'If you give something away to me, I will give you something less valuable in return.'**
- **'Just two or three minor things to clear up.' The interpretation would be, 'I am just about to ask you for something outrageous.'**
- **'What I am about to suggest will be to your advantage', meaning, 'My next concession is practically worthless to you.'**
- **'I think we are almost there', which translated means, 'I think I've got you and I would like to sign up rather quickly please.'**

These phrases and others like them tend to appear just before agreement, and can easily throw us off course. Beware of them and be ready for them. A simple catch-all reply can be 'I'm not sure about that, but if you... then we...'

Don't be afraid to make your counterpart work hard

The harder they work, the greater their satisfaction. How they got the deal they got is important. In this context, when about to say 'Yes', ask yourself what else you could achieve before agreeing. Don't rush into concluding, even if it is near. Develop a habit of waiting just before agreement is expressed and ask for a little more.

When you have finished you might say, 'You are a difficult person to persuade.' It verbalises respect and appreciation.

Do identify buying signals in your negotiations

Ideally the buyer needs to feel they have reached a decision independently of the seller, meaning the best presentation is one where the audience believe they have persuaded themselves. This can be achieved through careful structure. Salespeople use a technique called 'probe, confirm, match and close' and once they have completed that sequence they can use what marketers call the Classic Presentation Sequence (CPS). This is an expansion of match and close, and whether we are sales trained or not, we can use it:

1. The buyer presents the situation – why it is unsatisfactory and why it poses a real problem unless *handled at once*.

2. The buyer presents the implications of the problem and why it spells hidden and future problems too.
3. The seller presents the solution and why it meets the buyer's immediate needs with tangible benefits.
4. The seller presents the implications of the solution and why it offers hidden and future benefits too.
5. The seller conveys the urgency of obtaining the solution – what the buyer can lose by delaying and the extra benefits to be secured by acting now, eg 'Every day you delay this means...'
6. The benefits the buyer gains (in summary) balanced against the *low investment*.
7. The call to action – 'Give me the go ahead now and we will send you your first batch of leads this afternoon. In fact, if we could do this right now please, I can get on the phone for you and make some calls to some potential new customers for you.'

At the same time, beware of misinterpreting the signals from the seller. I once heard the following story in an event:

> In a train from Paris to Madrid, one compartment holds four people: a beautiful young girl travelling with her elderly grandmother, and an old stately general accompanied by a handsome young second-lieutenant. The foursome is sitting quietly as the train enters a tunnel in the Pyrenees. It is pitch dark in the tunnel when suddenly the sound of a loud kiss rings out followed by the even louder sound of a hard smack. When the train comes out the other end of the tunnel, the four people remain sitting silently without acknowledging the incident.
>
> The young girl thinks to herself, 'Boy I enjoyed the wonderful kiss the handsome lieutenant gave me. But my grandmother slapped him, so I don't suppose he will dare to try anything again in the next tunnel. Bother, why did she have to do that?' The grandmother thinks to herself, 'Why that fresh young man! He kissed my granddaughter! But I raised her properly and she responded by giving him a good hard slap. I'm proud of her, and I know he'll not try to kiss her in the next tunnel.' The general thinks to himself, 'I can't get over it. My aide went to one of the finest military schools, and I personally handpicked him. With all his

> training, he should have known better than to kiss that young girl. But in the dark, the girl obviously thought that it was me who kissed her, and I'm the one who got slapped. When we get back to the base, I'm going to give him a piece of my mind.' The young lieutenant thinks to himself: 'Gosh that was wonderful. How often do you get to kiss a beautiful girl and slap your boss at the same time!'

The moral of the story is that there is a great risk of reacting wrongly to what you think is a buying signal and an even greater risk of reacting to what we may perceive as a non-buying signal. Get the negotiating process right and you will not have to rely on signals – you will be driving a result. There are certain comments that signal definite interest and should be looked out for. The following remarks indicate that you are close to closing the sale:

- **How soon before we get the leads?**
- **What are the payment options?**
- **That seems a lot of money.**
- **That's a good point: I see what you mean.**
- **Can we take a trial?**
- **How much?**

One of my friends was in final negotiations with a world class car manufacturer. Towards the end when they were a little unsure how well it was going the counterpart asked my colleague if he would be willing to wear a different tie. My friend was a little nonplussed, he was wearing a quality suit and a decent tie and said a cautious, 'Yes, but why?' The counterpart said, 'In our business image is really important and to be honest your tie does not fit that bill, plus if you were to work for us we would want you to drive an xyz model for a month. The reason is simple, if you are going to work for us, you need to understand our passion, which is to design and build beautiful cars that people want to drive. The reality is you couldn't successfully work for us without genuinely understanding that passion.'

That was a clear buying signal and my colleague secured that piece of work. What is interesting to me is that he still drives the same make of car six years later. That's a definite win–win!

Look out for buying signals on the telephone

On the telephone we have the disadvantage of not being able to see the prospect and read their body language. Here are some buying signals possibly indicating that your counterpart is close to agreeing:

- **if they slow up, or quicken the pace of conversation;**
- **when their questioning becomes more frequent;**
- **when they loosen up, become more relaxed and less brusque or businesslike;**
- **when they react well to your trial close.**

Do look out for personality mirrors

Buyer or seller, consider this, does your prospect have a pet phrase they keep using? One prospect talked about his 'new regime', so the telesales executive used it constantly and won over a meeting. A computer sales director couldn't stop using the word 'environment', so the supplier's proposal used it a lot and won the sale.

Sensory language

NLP research has shown that there are three types of sensory language, and if we can match that used in the buyer's language, then the chances of a close are increased.

1. Visual – People who prefer visual information, eg 'I'll look it over', 'I see what you mean', 'It looks good to me', 'I'm seeing red'. Besides using visual words they speak very rapidly, and their tone of voice can be higher than average.
2. Auditory – People to whom the sounds are important, eg 'Speak to me', 'I'm tuned in to', 'Listen to this', 'I hear you',

'Let's discuss this', 'I question that'. They express themselves with a good command of language and speak in a rhythmic, melodious voice.

3. Feeling – People who use the sense of feeling, eg 'It feels to me like', 'I can't quite grasp it', 'I'm in touch with', 'I like', 'I'm not comfortable with', 'Let's get down to brass tacks'. They tend to talk slowly with lots of pauses and occasional sighs. Their voice tone is lower than average.

The importance of sensory language can be seen by looking at the phrase 'It's a nice day':

- **Visual – 'It's a beautiful day, looks like we will have some nice weather.'**
- **Auditory – 'I hear it's as clear as a bell today. The weather report sounded good.'**
- **Feeling – 'It feels wonderful today. I love a warm summer day.'**

Buyer or seller, you can have a surprising effect on someone when you use the sensory language they prefer. Listen for their language and mirror it back to them. Listen for the clues and mirror their language back.

Auditory	*Feeling*	*Visual*
hear	feel	picture
sounds	touch	look
tune in to	grasp	see
listen	comfortable	perspective
speak	excited	project
say	heavy	image
static	sharpen	preview
noise	tangible	show
accent	concrete	clarity
talk about	moves me	illustrate

Buyers and sellers use this table; you maybe even have a copy of it in your file. Use the words that your buyers use when you reply and in particular when you sum up specific points for agreement. Try also to match the pace of what they say.

Four specific techniques

Using social media in negotiation

The use of social media is a wonderful new tool in our negotiation skill set. Facebook is the most commonly known of the social media platforms but in essence is more tilted toward the domestic market. I am more likely to be David Oliver the dad and sailor, on Facebook, and less likely to be David Oliver international consultant and keynote speaker. Whereas on LinkedIn I am David Oliver the international consultant.

LinkedIn

How might I use LinkedIn? If you are going on a negotiation or fact-finding appointment, you might want to try personally inviting your prospect to join LinkedIn. You would do this personally, not in some mass e-mailing. Once they join your LinkedIn page you could look at their profile, select their contacts and see if there were any people you knew well that were mutual acquaintances. Then when it's appropriate you can ask a mutual acquaintance for a reference or where it's ethical some kind of information or some kind of positive posturing.

One of my clients needed to meet with the head of networking in a large computer reseller. Finding him on LinkedIn, he was able to identify two close contacts who were connected to him. Rather than use the LinkedIn template for requesting an introduction, he chose to e-mail his contacts, asking if they would be willing to introduce him. Both in turn contacted the prospect, and one called my client to advise on how best to positively approach the individual through reference to both personal and business interests.

My client fixed a meeting, to which he took two account managers and led a successful first stage in negotiations. Towards the end of the meeting he gained agreement for all to connect on LinkedIn and surprise surprise, the team were linked to a number of other key decision makers – I imagine you can guess what happened next: it opened up the door from this first-stage negotiation into several potential new sales visits. Double value.

We should also use LinkedIn and Twitter for research into our counterparts' own personal world and also into their company's world. This should be a standard part of our plan and prepare phase, to collate as much material as possible. Many companies have daily feeds to both Twitter and LinkedIn.

Google Alert

Google offer a fantastic free service called Google Alert. It's a godsend and an absolute must for all significant negotiations. Let's say you wanted to check out David Oliver and Insight Marketing before doing some kind of final or preparatory negotiation with us:

- **Simply search for 'Google Alert' on your browser, or**
- **On the Google homepage toolbar hit 'more', then hit 'even more'; there you will find the 'alert' icon. Click on**

that and set up the 'Search terms' you want to track and how, also the frequency!

- **Search terms are individual words or phrases – remember if you're searching an exact match use inverted commas at each end of the exact phrase you need, eg 'david oliver' or 'insight-marketing'. Google is not case sensitive.**
- **If you are looking for someone or something that has potentially millions of hits around the globe you probably need to use 'Search terms' in combination, eg 'david oliver' in combination with UK or USA.**

Google Alerts are great... find the right key words or phrases and you have free negotiation research 24/7/365. It never sleeps it just keeps coming; low effort, automated, non-stop negotiation intelligence, free.

Specific tips for negotiating print and promotion

Just about everyone in business – owner-manager, buyer and seller – gets involved in negotiating print and promotion. These tips may well help to reduce your costs and improve your end results.

When looking at negotiable variables or concessions, ask what if:

- **I prepare all the copy for the publication on your behalf?**
- **I supply all the text on CD or in electronic format?**
- **I collect the finished product (instead of a delivery charge)?**
- **I provide all photography?**
- **I buy the paper separately and supply to the printer?**
- **I provide all the page planning and structure of the publication?**

- **I could place this level of business regularly?**
- **I can introduce you personally to four other individuals who all place print at this kind of volume?**

Or you might say, 'I am an office supply company and would like to discuss supplying some office equipment in exchange for...'

Price rises – how to get it wrong

I was in my mid-twenties and had secured my biggest-ever negotiated deal to date, with a major international computer supplier. The deal was worth £3–4 million over a number of years. I was delighted with the deal, with the presentation we had made. I was particularly delighted with the warm relationships we had developed with the buying team. I was especially pleased too to have developed what I thought was a warm strategic relationship with the head of buying for Europe.

The work went well until, one fateful day following a price hike from our suppliers, we wrote to inform our customer that there was going to be an unavoidable price rise, to be put in force one month from now. By return I got the strongest letter imaginable from my favoured Head of Buying Europe. In it he put an immediate stop to all new business. He made it clear there was no way that they would tolerate this price rise. He equally made it clear that he felt he had been dealt with in a very shoddy manner.

He demanded to see me personally, and quickly. He was a shrewd and wise negotiator. When I went to see him he was his usual kindly self and we did agree a price rise eventually, although you don't need me to tell you that my aspirations were more than a little dented, and I did not achieve my target figure.

How should I have done it differently? Easy! I should have gently prepared the way with press articles, e-zines, and so on, to show the reality of global price increases with this market, these materials, etc. I should then have arranged a meeting to discuss urgently together how we could minimise the impact of these global trends. I should have researched, rehearsed and prepared, with my ideal outcome clearly in my head.

Do research before you buy

If you know what you want to buy and you know from whom you want to buy, then gather information first. Go with press cuttings, ring around to assess a broad range of prices. Go with printed special offers, go with price lists and say, 'I really want to buy from you; this is the price offered elsewhere.'

Gill Greenwood was buying two office desks. She shopped around and secured some competitive quotes. She rang up her preferred supplier and asked for a quotation. She was given a price of £375. She told the salesman that she had quotes for £275, what could he do? He came back some hours later and said, 'I can offer you a price of £275.' Gill said, 'I can give you the order for another £10 reduction on each.' She got the deal. Doesn't that show how just a few minutes on the phone can save you in this case £110 × 2? Just say you did that four times per month, ten months in the year. You have just added £8,800 to your profit.

Final words

The ones that nearly got away

Here are some powerful one-liners. Not comprehensive enough to make a chapter of their own, but add them up and be impressed!

Don't exaggerate facts. Don't 'elasticate' the hard information. Honesty and integrity always pay off in the end. Act dishonestly and you launch a boomerang. It has the uncanny ability of coming back and hitting you on the head!

Don't assume facts. Don't assume you have judged your counterpart's mood or feelings correctly – always check with W questions.

Be patient. Delay is always frustrating, but it is always better than a bad decision. Rushed decisions are usually bad for both parties.

If you are going to introduce extra terms or extra costs, have printed proof.

Don't believe everything you are allowed to hear. Check out the validity of any key information you are allowed to overhear.

The ten commandments

1. *Always ask for more*. It is a legitimate tactic to use 'The Shocker' with the opening offer. Remember to have clear reasons for the opening price. Those reasons must have credibility, they must appear to be legitimate.
2. *Never say yes first time* and never accept the first counter-offer.
3. *Don't succumb to price rot* – remember, it's a buyer's job to challenge all prices. It's the seller's job to ask for profitable prices. Don't forget that the whole of the free market economy is geared to have a downward-pressurising impact on price. For buyer and seller the rule is the same: don't succumb.
4. *Don't give away at the start that your position is negotiable*. If you use the phrase 'It is negotiable' – you have written the counterpart a blank cheque. It means you have already given away money. We should never do it.
5. *If concession is necessary, trade reluctantly*, and slowly.
6. *Don't ever change price without changing proposal*. When bargaining, use the magic phrase '*If you... then we...*' Ensure that you have a list of all your negotiable variables. Have at hand what can be changed and what its cost to you is.
7. *Watch bargaining activity just before a deadline*. If you imposed the deadline yourself, get higher authority to change it, if it becomes damaging to your negotiation. Always try to find your counterpart's deadlines or pressure points. Ask them what time constraints they are under. And use that information to build your authority.
8. *Avoid careless or unnecessary tough phrases*. It may well produce intransigence in your counterpart.
9. *Stop seeing price as the primary issue*. One of my friends is senior manager in a leading international forklift truck company. On one occasion he was responsible for a launch event. He negotiated a significantly lower price

from one supplier – particularly compared to the other competitors. In doing so he forced the supplier to cut corners, which seriously jeopardised the success of the event. It incurred other costs that he had to recover. He said to me that the key lesson for him was learning to recognise when you are forcing a supplier to compromise quality, simply to appease a price requirement. In his words, 'It is not always defeat to yield on price. In fact the reverse can be true!' It is important to remember that all the variables in and around the deal can be used to improve it. The danger for buyers is to try intuitively to give the seller tunnel vision that sees the price and little else. Avoid it. Keep looking at all the ingredients of the deal and keep the focus off price.

10. *Keep a sense of humour*. If you carry on too long and too intensely, the thing sours and one party will leave feeling that it has been a negative experience. Ultimately we are looking for agreement. Lighten the atmosphere, so that it does not become heavy. If you can't express normal humour in the process, you will not be as effective as you can be.

Don't be afraid to give

Negotiation for me is a fine balance. I don't want to be a Scrooge and I certainly have no desire whatever to rip people off. Equally, I want to get the best possible deal for my own companies and my own areas of responsibility. And I know that if I don't negotiate, I will never get the best deal. So how do we handle this year on year, particularly when relationships are, rightly, regarded as very important? One answer for me has been to give during the contract period. One ancient proverb says, 'A man's gift makes room for him.'

I do not give at the negotiation phase because, as we have seen together, it will be interpreted as weakness. And incidentally, it can be construed as a bribe.

I have one client who retains me monthly, and commissions me to run public seminars. I wanted to follow this particular piece of advice, so I have just given him two days totally free where I will train some of his clients and charge nothing. This is not a prospecting exercise for me, it is a genuine gift to my client with no strings attached. Why do that? I do it because the relationship with my client is the most important ingredient and this is a clear way of investing in the relationship at a time when it cannot be confused with the negotiation process.

Don't forget PREPBAR©

As you come to the end of this book, the easiest way to get these concepts drilled into everyday experience is to remember PREPBAR©. Remembering the acronym (maybe even putting it into your PDA or Filofax) is a way of helping your brain to structure any rehearsal that you may find yourself confronted with. If you have the book to hand, you can easily turn to an appropriate chapter that may refresh a forgotten concept or skill. If you don't have the book with you, at least you stand a chance of remembering a proven process and making a positive difference. Let me remind you of the acronym:

Plan and prepare.
Rehearse.
Explore and explain.
Propose.
Bargain.
Agree.
Review.

Follow all seven steps and you will likely get a great result!

How to eat the elephant

I hope this book has been an interesting and impacting read. But please don't put it down here. I promised you at the beginning that this book could easily add thousands – and for many of you tens of thousands – of pounds to your net profit.

But of course it never will. It is destined to fail, destined to be a disappointment. Why? Because you won't apply it, will you? Come on now, be honest, you are about to put this book away, aren't you?

You told yourself that you would try to apply some of these principles when you next got a chance. Don't kid yourself. Do something now and there is a chance that you will make some real money. Leave it and you never will.

Write down the five key things that you know intuitively will give you the greatest advantage immediately. Jot them down *now* in the space below:

1. ....

2. ....

3. ....

4. ....

5. ....

Please use these at the next possible opportunity. Promise me this. If they work for you, write down the next five and try them. Keep doing it and you will not only read, but begin to implement the keys of negotiating effectively.

Why did I call it 'how to eat the elephant'? Simply this – the only way to eat an elephant is to do it one bite at a time. In other words, any daunting or sizeable task is best done in bite-size chunks. This is sometimes called the five per cent rule. Try to implement 100 per cent at one go and you will get demotivated quickly. However, we know from experience that if you take five per cent of the material at a time, it is manageable. You are likely to make it work, and you are most likely to make money! Five ways is roughly five per cent.

Go on, do it now. Do it for yourself, for your company, for your family.

God bless you as you put these principles into practice.

Contact details

Maybe right now you would like the possibility of a first class negotiator helping you in a specific one-off negotiation. Or perhaps you would like information on audio training programmes, in-company training, or consultancy? Then call 44 (0)870 787 7404 or e-mail davido@insight-marketing.com for information with no obligation.

Negotiation workshops tailored to your company or department

David Oliver provides negotiation workshops tailored precisely to your market and your specific application or requirements.

Aimed at your salespeople, managers or buyers, these workshops should enable you to see an increase of 10 per cent in your annual net profit. In fact it is common to achieve substantially more:

- **Discover how to improve your profits.**
- **Learn new ways to protect your prices.**
- **Learn how to get the best possible deal every time.**
- **Learn how to increase your confidence in six critical areas.**
- **Learn how to identify tactics used against you.**
- **Learn how to prepare countermeasures that work for you.**
- **Learn how to avoid giving too much away and discover how to know.**
- **Discover how and when to move in your negotiations.**
- **Explore how to move.**

Telephone +44 (0)870 787 7404 for an information pack and an MDSA© development toolkit totally free and without any obligation.

For audio training CDs with David Oliver presenting this material please go to the following website:

www.insight-marketing.com/negotiation_training

For a schedule of David's public events and webinars please e-mail enquiries@insight-marketing.com

Appendix

Here are some exercises that will help you put some of the ideas in this book into your world.

Negotiable variables

List your negotiable variables, or tradeables and then list how much they cost and what the value is to the client.

Take into account delivery, service, after sales, guarantees, warranties, volume, terms, etc.

Negotiable variables	Cost	Value to client

Put it in writing!

List below in the left-hand column what you should put in writing, and in the right-hand column what you actually do!

What should I put in writing	What I do (yes or no)

What do you give away?

Think about what you have given away or conceded in previous negotiations. List them below in the left-hand column. In the right-hand column, comment on how you could have charged, traded or handled it differently.

What I did	What I could have done